I0809966

boucherie

LOUISIANA TRUE books tell the stories of the state's iconic places, traditions, foods, and objects. Each book centers on one element of Louisiana's culture, unpacking the myths, misconceptions, and historical realities behind everything that makes our state unique, from above-ground cemeteries to zydeco.

PREVIOUS BOOKS IN THE SERIES

Mardi Gras Beads

Brown Pelican

Mardi Gras Indians

Po'Boy

Gumbo

Boudin

boucherie

CHASE CORMIER

Louisiana State University Press
Baton Rouge

Published by Louisiana State University Press
lsupress.org

LSU Press Paperback Original
Manufactured in the United States of America
First printing

Designer: Barbara Neely Bourgoyne
Typeface: Source Sans Variable
Printer and binder: Integrated Books International (IBI)

The manufacturer's authorized representative in the EU for product safety is Mare Nostrum Group B.V., Doelen 72, 4831 GR Breda, The Netherlands. Email: gpsr@mare-nostrum.co.uk.

Cover illustration: AdobeStock/Eric Isselée (modified)

Cataloging-in-Publication Data are available from the Library of Congress.
ISBN 978-0-8071-8723-4 (pbk.: alk. paper) — ISBN 978-0-8071-8774-6 (pdf) —
ISBN 978-0-8071-8773-9 (epub)

contents

boucherie

1

The Birth of a Butcher

It's summertime. I'm a teen in my hometown of Opelousas, Louisiana, heading on my bike to my grandfather's store, Kelly's Country Meat Block & Diner, to meet my grandparents for lunch. My grandfather has owned and operated Kelly's since 1970. It's located in a strip mall on State Highway 182, which goes through downtown Opelousas, heads south through Sunset, and then snakes its way farther down to Lafayette.

After a fifteen-minute ride, I arrive. I pedal my bike across a grassy area behind the store and then walk it through the gravel parking lot reserved for employees. A dumpster, a cardboard box smasher, a row of thirty-something store-n-lock units, a massive propane tank, and a trailer in which a longtime butcher lives all decorate the strip mall's less-seen rear exterior. I lay my bike down on the pavement behind Kelly's and walk past freight-containers-turned-freezers holding deer and hog meat from last winter, turkeys and hams of varying sizes for Thanksgiving, and boxes of frozen corn, sweet-potato patties, lima beans, ham hocks, and smoked turkey necks. I offer a "What's up y'all" greeting to a huddle of employees on their brief, daily cigarette break that follows the lunch-hour rush before passing a tin-walled and wood-floored warehouse used for dry storage, another freezer on the right, and an outdoor kitchen on the left. As I approach the back entrance to the building, the patchwork of cement slabs and their darkening degrees of gray beneath my feet indicate a gradual and constant growth outward as the meat market has become more and more successful over the decades. Finally, I pass a walk-in cooler and a metal building dedicated to sausage making before opening the big gray backdoor. I am struck by a wall of cold, conditioned air and the cry of a busy bandsaw.

I salute the working butchers to my right and turn left into the not-so-busy kitchen. The daily lunch rush has dwindled to a sort of autopiloted buzz of dishwashing, burger dressing, and the occasional plate-lunch fixing as salt-spangled French fries maintain their crispiness beneath a hot lamp. The women in the kitchen greet me with a smiley "Hey, Chase" and add a few extra *a*'s to my first name for good measure. I chat them up briefly while fixing my own plate. I scoop two big spoonfuls of long-grain rice (not my favorite, but this is a price-conscious restaurant after all, and long grain is cheaper than medium grain) from the rice steamer onto my plastic plate. Then I turn around to the wide stove populated by various Magnalite pots containing brown and rusty red gravies swimming with stewed meats and sausages and smaller pots filled with field peas, green beans, corn maque choux, smothered okra, and candied yams. It is a Monday, so my options are the usual red beans and rice or smothered steak in a brown gravy—a heavily spiced ragout made by browning sirloin steaks in a pot and then creating a gravy by deglazing the pot with onions and peppers. I go for the smothered steak. I spoon out plenty of dark-brown gravy and a tender piece of sirloin, placing them atop my pile of rice. I then add two steaming piles of field peas and sweet potatoes to the plate, as well as a dinner roll, and grab a chocolate chip cookie that I hold in my hand along with silverware, so as not to mix dessert with the pool of gravy on my plate. I leave small talk and service behind me as I make my way to a nearly full dining room where the clinking of silverware trebles the constant hum of lunch-break chitchat.

I set my plate down at the first table on the right, the usual family table, and join my grandmother Elaine Cormier, my grandfather Kelly Cormier, and his childhood friend, a retired priest from Richard, Louisiana, who often joins them for their late lunch. We talk about what I've been up to, how the lunch service went for them today, the weather. As they settle into the conversation, they share stories of yesteryear, like how digging sweet potatoes often left them with hands covered in relentlessly sticky sap and a sore back from bending to dig up the sweet tubers and then standing to load them into a wagon drawn either by a mule or a couple of strong siblings. All this under the late-summer Louisiana sun on a shadeless prairie somewhere outside the hamlet of Church Point. I listen, captivated by the details and dashes of comedy used to flavor and ease the harsh realities of a bygone era. I take a bite of syrup-sweetened yams that instantly cools my mouth from the well-spiced brown gravy. The conversation moves on to more current affairs as we empty our plates and shift into dessert and coffee mode.

Eventually, the conversations fade, we clear the table, and we all go our separate ways. We shake the hand of the priest as he stands and wishes us a good afternoon, and my grandfather goes to the back office to count the day's earnings and prepare a bank deposit. My grandmother dedicates herself to refilling the cash register, deep-cleaning the counter space and fountain drink area, and other tasks. I decide to go and spend some time with the butchers in the meat market next door.

Have you ever watched someone who has mastered their craft? Here, butchers work with seemingly thoughtless precision. They move with the same intention and grace as skilled painters standing before a canvas, offering the slightest gestures with their brushes, and following lines that only they can see. The butchers' knives are extensions of their will, as they stand over the horizontal canvas, the white plain of a cutting board stained with splashes of crimson and gelatinous globs of creamy fat. Mysterious seasonings powder the tabletops and floors. They carve, trim, debone, filet, and slice their way toward something that will soon resemble food. Right now, they are preparing for tonight's batch of smoked sausage. As on any other afternoon outside the holiday season or the arrival of gumbo weather, they need to debone and cut up 300 pounds of Boston butt pork shoulders, which will then be ground into sausage meat and mixed well with black pepper, cayenne, paprika, and curing salt. This mixture then has to be stuffed into sausage casings and hung in double links on wheeled racks to be rolled into a smoker, where they will spend most of the night enveloped in a thick, warm cloud of hickory, pecan, and oakwood smoke.

The entrance to Kelly's Country Meat Block and Diner before it was sold in 2018.

I began working at Kelly's as a dishwasher in the summer of 2014. Summers are slow in the meat market, but there are always dishes to wash, floors to sweep and mop, walls to scrub, and things to organize. Summers are for deep cleaning and selling meat to be barbecued. Today, as I write this, my memory's eye sees me standing in black, nonslip shoes purchased at Wal-Mart, with a wide stance to avoid slipping, and my hips leaning against the deep industrial-sized three-sectioned stainless-steel sink. I am wearing jeans, a blue Kelly's shirt, a red apron, and a baseball cap. To my left is a pile of dirty plastic lugs, metal pans, bowls, knives, spoons, and rags. In front of me is a sink half full of soapy dishwater in which I use various white rags to wash and chip away at the hill of plastic and stainless steel, moving the dishes toward my right where I sanitize, rinse, and dry them before finally stacking them either on an overhead shelf or in their designated places behind me.

When I first arrive at work, I decide whether the parking lot needs tidying up. If so, I am out front with a gas-powered backpack leaf blower before sunrise, picking up trash and blowing the asphalt. Before the dishes pile up, I sweep and mop the market floors, the cooler floors (but not, of course, the freezer floor), and the outdoor cookroom floors. I scrub walls, wipe the windows and display glass on coolers, dust the counters, and stock the front walk-in cooler.

You need to understand the importance of the 400-square-foot display cooler, located near the front door. It is mostly full of specialty items in overfilled trays, so that customers can see what Kelly's offers that is ready to be bagged, weighed, priced, and purchased. In that case, from left to right, are smoked pork sausage, fresh pork sausage, stuffed and seasoned pork chops, whole hams and picnic hams, whole turkey breasts, pork ribs, pork ham roasts seasoned and stuffed with a spicy garlic blend, boneless chicken breasts seasoned and wrapped in bacon, whole fryers seasoned and unseasoned, whole hens, smoked tasso, smoked ham hocks, smoked turkey necks, smoked chicken halves, smoked pork spareribs, and an exclamation point of smoked andouille. In addition to washing dishes and cleaning the market, I was also responsible for washing this display case daily and keeping it full. The goal was to offer an overflowing exhibition of specialty items and to keep some of every meat product there, so meat cutters could quickly grab them without having to go into one of the bigger coolers in the back. The frozen spectacle was equally impressive and included stuffed chickens, crawfish tails from the Atchafalaya Basin, gumbo crabs (smaller boiled and frozen crabs used in seafood gumbo), jumbo lump crabmeat, claw meat, and an array of soups ready to defrost and warm up in pint-sized containers, including corn and crab soup, duck and andouille gumbo, and broccoli and cheese soup.

Once the parking lot is clean, floors are mopped and swept, and the display coolers and freezers and front walk-in cooler are all as packed with meat as can be, I wash the dishes. As I stand facing the industrial-sized sink, most of the action is happening behind me. After I knock down the pile of dishes, I get back to bringing in boxes of meat to fill the coolers. To effectively maintain full, well-organized meat cases and coolers, I need to learn about the different cuts of meat and parts of the animal. I need to know not only what a pork loin looks like but also how to hang this slippery, 75-pound piece of meat, fat, and bone on a stainless-steel hook. Beef rounds are heavier still, weighing between 100 and 200 pounds each: I must hang one of these in the walk-in cooler a certain way so that the butchers can smoothly grab it each time a customer orders a round steak.

Soon I start to help some of the butchers with orders by bagging cut-up fryer chickens and turkey necks, talking with customers, and fulfilling orders with products that do not need to be cut

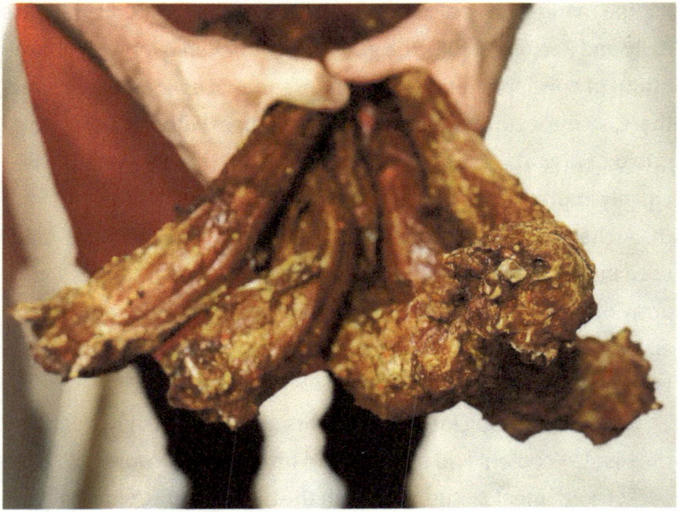

A butcher at Kelly's holds a bouquet of smoked turkey necks to be cut into chunks for a gumbo.

on the bandsaw—like five-pound boxes of smoked sausage, whole smoked ham hocks, marinated pork cubes (or *grillades*), seasoned pork chops stuffed with sausage meat, and chicken breasts seasoned and wrapped in bacon.

I can also sell ground meat on my own. If a customer comes in and asks for some ground beef, I go to the walk-in cooler, grab a piece of beef chuck, bring it to the butcher block, take *my* knife (each butcher has his own knife), cut a piece of meat that looks like the weight the customer wanted, run it through the meat grinder two times, bag it, make sure it is the right weight, type in the price per pound, walk back to the front counter to ask the customer if they want anything else, check them out, and send them on their way.

Eventually I realize that I need to learn how to use the big bandsaw. It occupies the central part of the work area where all the steaks, roasts, chickens, and turkey necks—indeed, anything else that cannot be cut with a knife—are cut. I spend a lot of time around this saw while bagging chicken parts, and I grew up walking past the loud, screaming hunk of stainless steel. Finally, the time comes for me to operate it. For my first cut, I choose a frozen turkey neck. I stand with my nonslip shoes spread wide, on a firm foundation, hold the footlong smoked neck at each end, and slide it forward to let the vertical descending bandsaw split it easily in two. Phew. Not so bad.

Before long I am cutting smoked turkey necks, fryer chickens, hens for gumbo, and pork chops like I was born for it. One day, a customer orders a few smoked ham hocks that need to be cut; they are frozen and about the size and shape of a fist. Suddenly, when I lean against the saw, a familiar anxiety rises in me as I realize that my fingers need to go uncomfortably close to the saw so that the serrated blade can run through the middle of the hock. It is possible to do so, of course; all the other butchers do it. What makes me nervous is that all these butchers, at some point, have expressed the fear they feel while cutting these hard, rolly knuckle-shaped hocks. Some of them have already told me stories of the serrated blade catching a piece of ham bone and taking the hock for a tumbling ride, swallowing it down into where the banded blade goes. I fire up the saw, think about the worst-case scenario, and go for it, nerves and all. I focus on my fingertips and hold the hock against the shelf of the saw top and slide it forward. So far, so good. We cut these hocks into quarters, so I must pull the two halves back, turn them 45 degrees, press them together, and hold the split hock on the ends like you would hold a Subway sandwich, and give it one more slide to slice it crossways.

With each success comes more confidence in operating the bandsaw. Soon I am cutting everything with youthful assertiveness, my curiosity freely feeding my ability. I cut ribeye steaks, sirloin steaks, tenderloin steaks, pork steaks, pork chops, beef and pork ribs, fryer chickens and hens, and even big strips of pork belly to be cubed and cooked later as cracklings. One landmark accomplishment that led to my grandfather congratulating me was fulfilling my first order of what Kelly's called a "fifty-pound bundle." This is one of the most economical meat bundles that we offer and is especially popular around the time that people receive their monthly benefits; these are funds provided electronically by the Louisiana Department of Children & Family Services to low-income households to help them feed their families. Our fifty-pound bundle offers a wide variety of high-quality meat at a very fair price. It consists of ten pounds of ground beef chuck, ten pounds of pork chops, ten pounds of pork (shoulder) steaks, ten pounds of 7-steaks (beef shoulder), and ten pounds of chicken leg quarters. The precision and efficiency with which I cut, weigh, price, wrap, bag, and process this order mark a turning point in my becoming a butcher at Kelly's, and my ability to successfully fulfill this order serves as a doorway through which I pass from apprentice into the world of a butcher.

Promotional artwork on the façade of Kelly's Meat Block.

What set Kelly's apart from other meat sellers was that it did not offer one- and two-pound packages of ground meat; precut and prepackaged ribeye steaks, sirloin steaks, tenderloin steaks, New York strips, pork chops, and pork steaks; and other smaller, preportioned cuts of meat sitting in Styrofoam trays and wrapped in plastic wrap. Kelly's way of doing business was a response to a meat industry that was moving toward efficiency, packageability, and ease but that also minimized and ultimately eliminated interaction between the customer and the meat cutter. Kelly's answer was to offer nothing precut, instead letting the customer request steaks cut to order and meat ground to order. Except for some specialty items, all meat products were portioned and personalized according to customer needs. The Kelly's business model indeed went against the mass-market, high-efficiency, get in and get out, relatively low-profit modern retail model. Kelly's celebrated customer–butcher communication and a humanized meat purchasing experience were reminiscent of meat markets in early twentieth-century sharecropping communities across south Louisiana.

My grandfather Kelly Cormier grew up in Richard, Louisiana, in the 1940s and 1950s, when most people did not have refrigeration in their homes. Like others growing up then, he mostly ate beans and other vegetables that his family grew. But to ensure a diet sufficient in protein, the Cormiers also had to raise, kill, and process livestock. My grandfather and his family always had several pigs, a few head of cattle, and plenty of chickens and guinea fowl. On Sundays the family would come together to eat a round steak in a brown gravy, chicken in a gravy, or smothered pork chops.

In addition to boucheries—communal gatherings of families from a rural community to kill and process pigs to provide enough meat to sustain them through the winter—people in these communities could also rely on their neighborhood meat market, known in French as a *halle.* For example, when my grandfather was a child, his animal-based protein principally came from poultry and from pigs killed in communal boucheries. When cows were killed and processed, the beef would be kept in a communal *halle,* where the community butcher would store meat for a fee. The *halle* was like a community fridge or a co-op meat-processing and storage operation. In the *halle* was a *glacière*—a box big enough to walk into that stored block ice, hung front- and hindquarters, and smaller cuts of beef wrapped in thick butcher paper.

The local butcher thus played a vital role in the community's ability to access meat. Every time people wanted to pick up a piece of beef that was being stored at the community meat market, they needed to go and interact with the butcher there. Therefore, socializing with the butcher was a central part of the meat-purchasing experience. The weekly ritual of cooking rich stews, gravies, and sauces also included chatting with the local butcher, catching up on local happenings and gossip, and exchanging family news and even recipes. The *halle* was thus a communal node of communication linked directly to food.

Today, a few specialty meat markets—for example, Paul's Meat Market in Ville Platte and the Superette in Eunice—still use the butcher–customer, blast-from-the-past approach to selling meat, but that business model is quickly disappearing. Even before Kelly's

Country Meat Market & Diner was sold in 2018, it began moving to a precut, prepackaged approach to selling meat. To counter this trend and as part of the farm-to-table craze, local farms now offer whole hogs and chickens with the option of processing them for customers. For example, T-Moise Farms in Sunset, Louisiana, specializes in "All-Natural, Pasture-Raised Berkshire Pork, Grass-Fed & Grass-Finished Beef, Pasture-Raised Poultry & Eggs, and Raw Honey" but mainly sells its products to restaurants and at farmers' markets.

My grandfather's decision in 2018 to sell Kelly's surprised its employees and me. I had only been working there about four years, but some of the butchers had been cutting meat on that saw since the 1980s. There was a sudden and jolting decline in morale. With my future in meat cutting now uncertain, I decided that summer to quit my job as a butcher and enroll in the University of Louisiana at Lafayette's (ULL) graduate program in Francophone studies; there I would also teach French courses to undergraduate students and receive a very modest stipend to go toward my tuition. I knew the professors and was aware of that program and its dedication to the French language and Francophone culture in my home state, having graduated from ULL the summer before. Instead of working as a meat cutter, I decided to conduct research about butchering in Louisiana and would go on to write my doctoral dissertation on the boucherie.

The book you are reading draws from my doctoral research and provides a history of changing cultural patterns related to communal boucherie practices over the past century. Here are some of the major stages of development in the ritual's evolution since the early twentieth century:

- At the turn of the twentieth century, most rural community members participated in the raising and butchering of domesticated animals, taking part in communal home boucheries.
- In the early to mid-twentieth century, rural farmers raised and butchered their own animals but paid a local butcher to store their meat in a refrigerated *halle* and ordered custom cuts of their choice whenever desired.
- By the turn of the twenty-first century, few raised their own animals. People purchased meat in a machine-packaged and mass-marketed form, and many did not know which part of the animal they were buying or eating or where it was sourced. Consumers seldom interacted with a butcher; only a few traditional country butcher shops continued to operate in rural Louisiana.
- Today, boucheries are experienced only as ritual celebrations where attendees likely do not witness or participate in the killing, butchering, processing, or cooking of any animals; nor do they know much about the parts or preparation of the feast. Yet these modern boucheries somehow help create and reinforce the essential cultural identity of attending "Cajuns."
- In the twenty-first century, the farm-to-table trend is popular at restaurants and farmers' markets, but custom meat processing is rarely available to typical consumers. Only a few individuals have the requisite opportunities, resources, or traditional skills to perform the traditional boucherie of a century ago. Families are smaller and often dispersed, and neighborhoods are less in-

teractive and cohesive. Today's communities are structurally, socially, and culturally different from those of a century past—and so are the "Cajuns."

In the following chapters, I examine the evolution of the state's butchering practices from their beginnings with the lower Mississippi Delta's first inhabitants, who lived about 12,000 years ago, to the colonial days, into statehood, and throughout the modern period, leading up to today's boucherie tradition. I investigate various sociocultural developments along the way, as well as the impact on the boucherie of Indigenous butchers; French, Spanish, and German immigrants; Acadian, West African, and Caribbean foodways; Americanization; Cajunization; and recent shifts toward a more plant-based diet. I explore early colonial travel journals, cookbooks, television shows (like *New Orleans Cooking with Kevin Belton* and *Bizarre Foods with Andrew Zimmern*), and many other texts and media to study this rich tradition. The road toward this project has led to many enlightening encounters and discussions with butchers, cooks, eaters, and scholars.

The evolution of the boucherie tells a story of immigration, colonization, multicultural exchange, survival, adaptation, and celebration. After putting down the knife and picking up the pen, it is my pleasure to share with you some of my most noteworthy findings gleaned from my years studying the boucherie in Louisiana, a ritual that is as much about conservation as it is about conversation.

2

Where Meat Comes From

My unique relationship to butchering—as a meat cutter and as a researcher but, more importantly, as a member of a family that proudly lives our Cajun heritage—has transformed my understanding of the boucherie. I grew up going to boucheries and hearing about them; as a consumer-participant, I had a different understanding of the ritual than I do today as a scholar of Louisiana cultural studies. Before diving into the particularities of the boucherie's wide array of sociocultural influences, let me provide a more synthesized description of a boucherie.

Typically, throughout history, boucheries were held out of necessity, to ensure nourishment and survival in small rural communities. The events are organized so that each household in a community takes its turn hosting the boucherie and supplying the pig(s) to be slaughtered. Authors and scholars often emphasize the egalitarian nature of events like boucheries, coups de main, and cochons de lait (pig roasts).

A sign indicates where the action is happening.

The boucherie begins, usually very early on a Saturday morning, with the killing of one or more pigs. Those assigned to meat cutting quickly drain the blood, mix it with salt in a bowl, and stir it to prevent coagulation. The blood is used later for *boudin noir* (blood sausage). Participants then remove the fur from the pig. This process involves a drum/barrel filled with hot water used to scald the pigs, either by rolling them around inside the drum of water or by laying burlap sacks on them and pouring the water onto them to soften the skin and make scraping the fur with hands and knives much easier. The meat cutters proceed to slit the animal's belly longitudinally from throat to tail and remove the organs. Once all the entrails are taken out, they remove the head and feet before they skin and cut up—or quarter—the animal into manageable pieces (two hindquarters, two front quarters, and one backbone). Traditionally, men readied and slaughtered the animal, removed the entrails, and cut up both the meat and entrails, while women gathered indoors to prepare for sausage production. This entailed cleaning the pig intestines by turning them inside out and scrubbing them with water and baking soda. (I focus on pigs here, but beef entrails were also used.) Once cleaned, the intestines were used both as casings and as stuffing for boudin, andouille, and sausage. This gendered division of labor separated the men from the women—men worked outside, while women worked inside—but through their cooperative participation, validated their roles within their community and household.

Butchers remove the fur from a pig in the early stages of a family boucherie in Maurice, Louisiana.

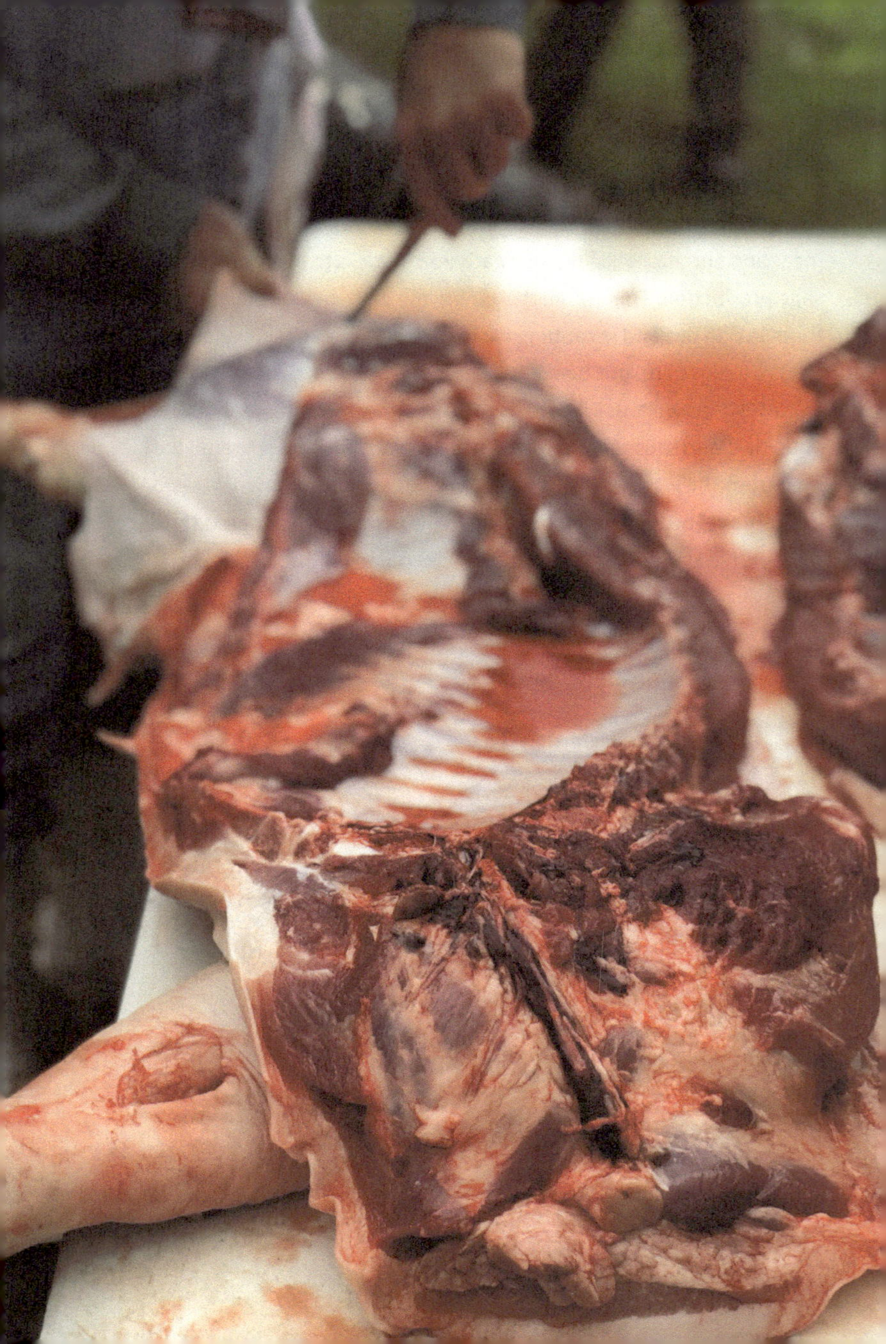

Pork ribs waiting to be cut into pieces and boiled in oil for a mid-morning snack: fried ribs.

Opposite: The butchers work with filet knives to split the pig halves into quarters.

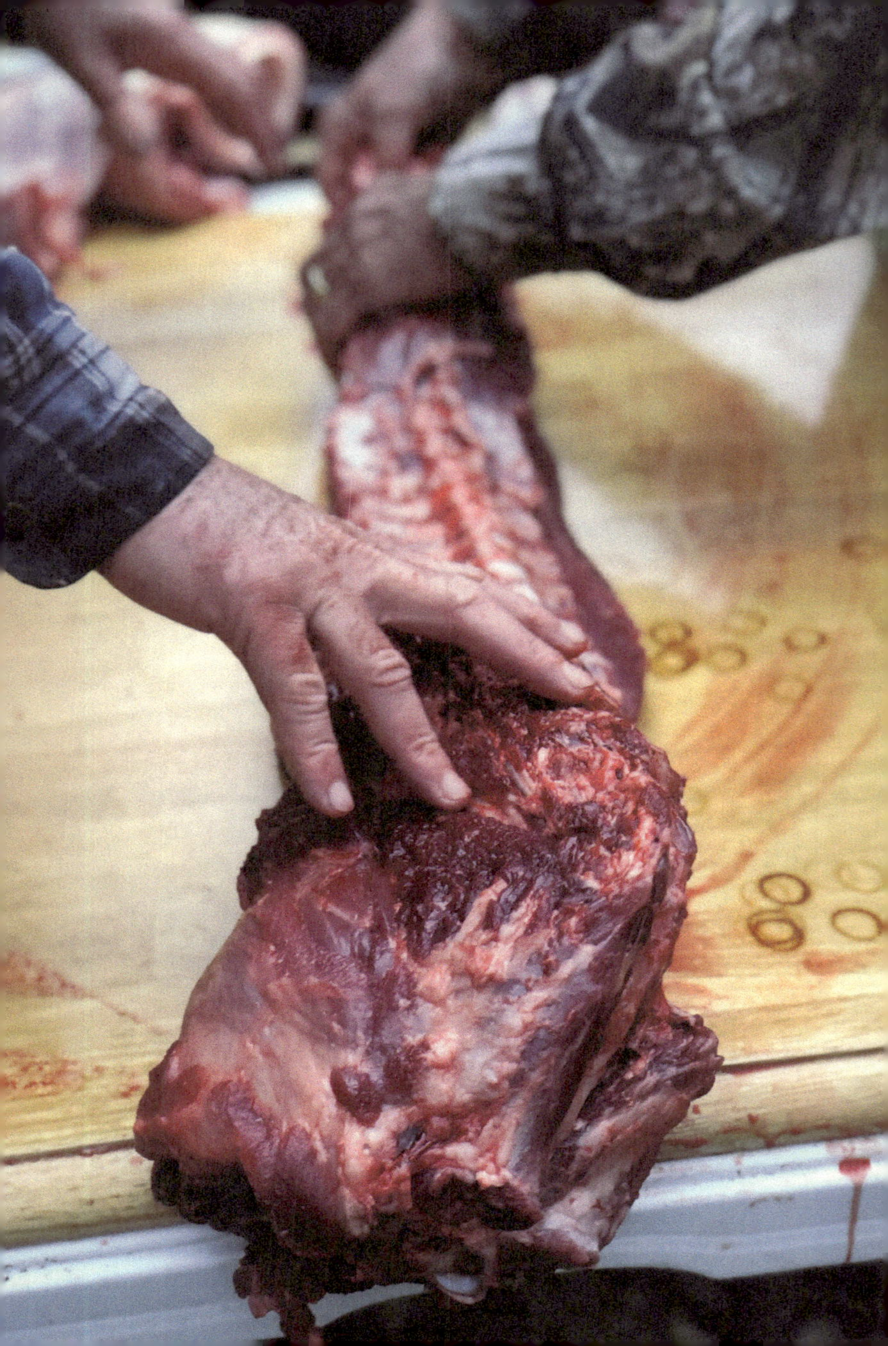

A man seasons pork backbone steaks with salt, red pepper, and paprika.

Opposite: The butchers work together to prepare and cut the pork loin into pieces for backbone stew.

Most of the meat from the animal (the shoulders and hindquarters) was used for boudin and sausage stuffing. For the sausage, this meat would be ground and mixed with a spice blend of ground cayenne pepper and salt. For the boudin, the meat and organs—lungs, kidneys, brain, spleen, pancreas, liver—were mixed with rice, ground peppers, and salt. Some of the meat mixture would also be stuffed into the stomach (also called the ponce or chaudin), which was sewn shut and sometimes smoked along with the sausages in a smokehouse or perhaps in a small wooden structure—usually a chicken coop or sweet-potato curing house—that was converted into a temporary smokehouse. In addition to smoking, a pickling solution of coarse salt and rendered fat, called *saumure,* was used to preserve smoked meats. Meats would be placed in heavy crock containers, often called "jars," with the *saumure* and kept for weeks in a cool place, such as on the north-facing porch of the house or in a sack in the family cistern. The head and feet were boiled to make hog's head cheese, reminiscent of French country pâté.

The purpose of this complicated process was to preserve as much meat as possible and to provide cheap and accessible protein throughout the winter to community members, who lived primarily on the vegetables they grew, such as sweet potatoes, beans, and corn. Through the preservation of meat, the boucherie also preserved the community, its members, and its traditions. For centuries, it also helped people in Louisiana conserve—whether money, resources, food, cultural markers, identity, or ways of life.

Since the 1950s, when refrigeration technology was introduced to the region, the boucherie has taken on different forms, but many follow the traditional processes just described. They pay homage to the tradition, celebrate Louisiana foodways, and provide a venue where friends and family can gather during Carnival season or simply to party. The modern boucherie focuses more on the preservation of foodways, cultural identity, and a pastoral ideal and less on the preservation of meat, which is now usually cooked and consumed the same day that the animals are killed. Yet, contemporary boucheries produce many of the same traditional smoked, salted, and pickled foods, such as cracklings, smoked sausage, hog's head cheese, and boudin. Such items can be found in gas stations, meat markets, grocery stores, and convenience stores all over south Louisiana today.

The ways that the meat is prepared today—whether as backbone stew, débris (or cowboy stew), fried ribs, pork shoulder in a brown gravy, smothered sausage, and so on—are similar to how the preserved meat in earlier boucheries was prepared in the weeks following the ritual. Thus, contemporary boucheries follow the same rituals but condense them into one day of nostalgic festivities, modified to meet the demand for speed in our twenty-first-century society. Yet, unlike the traditional boucherie in which all attendees participated, contemporary boucheries are primarily a spectator sport. Often a small crew of butchers kill and process the meat, while the rest of the attendees observe or provide entertainment through music or other means.

Of course, the boucherie, like any sustained cultural event, has taken on many forms throughout its history and throughout the region. However, the foods Louisianans eat today—with the exception of fast and processed foods and the wide availability of imported foods—have largely gone unchanged since the Archaic Period. Our reliance on these Indigenous food practices is evident in the modern American food system. For example, sustainable corn cultivation echoes the "three-sisters" method (corn, beans, squash). Furthermore, smoking and drying as preservation methods and wild-harvested foods like salmon and berries are still present in the US food industry. People have participated in boucheries—though called by different names—in Louisiana since the ancestors of the Indigenous inhabitants arrived in the Lower Mississippi Valley around 12,000 years ago.

Indigenous Boucherie

Archaeological data tell us that nomadic big-game hunters first began migrating to the region known today as Louisiana during the Paleoindian Period (12,500–9,200 BC). Toward the end of the last Ice Age, when large ice sheets extended as far south as present-day Illinois, groups of North American hunters and gatherers entered Louisiana, most likely via the Mississippi River Valley, in search of food in a climate that was marginally cooler than that of today. For most of Louisiana's anthropological history, people survived by hunting and gathering. In addition to the bountiful fruits, vegetables, nuts, and berries that grew in the humid, subtropical climate, they hunted thirteen-foot-tall woolly mammoth and mastodon, enormous bison, twelve-foot-tall sloths, horses, and peccary (pig-like mammals).

Like pigs, peccaries notoriously eat virtually anything. Unlike their evolutionary cousins such as cows, giraffes, goats, and sheep—which sought open grasslands about ten million years after the extinction of dinosaurs—peccaries and pigs remained forest dwellers, surviving on nuts, fruits, roots, tubers, fungi, tender leaves, insects, and meat; they even followed humans around to feed on their food scraps. Their simple digestive systems and multipurpose teeth allowed them to adapt to nearly any situation. The evolutionary lines of the two families—pigs (Suidae) and peccaries (Tayassuidae)—split in Asia about thirty-five million years ago. Eventually, peccaries migrated to the Western Hemisphere, and humans, recognizing their adaptability and culinary value, followed peccaries and other edible mammals all over North and South America. According to J. Ashley Sibley, mid-twentieth-century excavations suggest that the killing, processing, and consumption of peccaries took place at what is now Avery Island during the Paleoindian Period, as well as at Tunica Bayou in 9,540 BC and at Jones Creek from 4,380 to 200 BC. However, subsequent studies by Kurt M. Wilson and Matthew G. Hill reject some of the findings at Avery Island and at Tunica Bayou, stating that no reliable data connect human–peccary interaction in Louisiana.

Nonetheless, it is fair to claim that people have been coming together to kill, process (remove fur, entrails, bones, fat, and meat from the carcass), preserve, and cook mammals for millennia. Archaeological finds provide the oldest evidence of boucheries in Louisiana's history that apparently did not involve peccaries. Recent oral histories and food writing, like *Choctaw Food* by Ian Thompson, tell us that butchering was a major part of Louisiana Indigenous cultures and that Louisiana humans were old hands at hunting and butchering by the Late Pleistocene. To the many generations that would follow them, Paleoindian populations communicated how they lived, survived, and expressed themselves through foodways and material culture.

Anthropologists mark the transition from the Paleoindian Period to the Archaic Period by the extinction of all large terrestrial mammals in North America except for bears and buffalo, and the advent of a significantly warmer, drier climate. Therefore, what people were eating drastically changed in the Archaic Period. They gradually developed more sophisticated gathering techniques, especially in coastal areas and waterways where resources were more plentiful. However, these individuals still relied heavily on fauna for protein throughout the entire Archaic Period and the eras that followed. As natural levees, grasslands, and other elevated areas developed, Louisiana supported an even larger variety of animal life than in the Paleoindian Period. Bears, buffalos, deer, wild turkeys, raccoons, squirrels, opossums, otters, rabbits, foxes, wild cats, and muskrats were among the hunted animals inhabiting the Lower Mississippi Valley during the Archaic Period. As Sibley notes, the semi-nomadic people no longer had to migrate in search of big game, relying more on dependable sources of food, such as shellfish and other seafood, deer, wild turkey, and black bear, which were all drawn to the prolific Mississippi Delta.

Beginning around 1000 BC during the Woodland Period, the ancestors of the Choctaw, Natchez, and other Louisiana tribes relied to a greater degree on horticulture, developed pottery, built elaborate ceremonial mounds, and gathered varieties of roots, berries, and seeds. Eventually, maize became a dominant part of the diet, and domestication of some animals began during later periods. Yet, according to Nancy W. Hawkins and Robert W. Neuman, the hunting of animals for meat remained important throughout prehistory.

What we call "living sustainably" today hardly compares to how prehistoric groups of people lived. For most of Louisiana's history, people sustained themselves, the land, and animal life by living as one part of nature among many. Humans likely did not consider themselves at the center of nature. During prehistoric times, there seemed to be a shared notion that humans and their environment had to cultivate a reciprocal relationship because people depended on the survival of other animals, plants, waterways, and the land to sustain them.

When I conducted research on the history of meat processing, it was a privilege to discover and access some very enlightening sources. For example, in *Prehistoric Indian Settlements of the Changing Mississippi River Delta,* William G. McIntire writes that in the Archaic Period, "Bear flesh was dried and eaten; the oil or fat was often used in food preparation and the skin for covering." This is the first reference I found to two essential components of the boucherie: the preservation of meat and the rendering of fat. Therefore, more than 7,500 years before the arrival of Europeans in Louisiana, Native people of the Lower Mississippi Valley were coming together to kill and process buffalos, bears, deer, peccaries, and other terrestrial mammals for their meat, fat, and skin to survive as a collective.

Centuries later, French Canadian fur traders René-Robert Cavelier, Sieur de La Salle, his lieutenant Henri de Tonti, and several other men set off down the Mississippi River in February 1682. On April 9 of that year, La Salle reached the river's mouth and claimed the river and its drainage basin for France and King Louis XIV. In 1698, when Pierre

Le Moyne d'Iberville was sent to Louisiana by the French Crown to establish a military outpost near the mouth of the Mississippi River, he encountered many Native tribes occupying the Mississippi Delta. He and his campmates desperately depended on these tribes' resources for their sustenance. As Daniel H. Usner notes, by the end of the seventeenth century Louisiana was home to more than 70,000 Native Americans and many distinct tribes and nations.

Throughout much of that century, France was overextended across several continents and was facing food shortages; as a result, French settlers living in Louisiana received little to no aid from their homeland. In 1699, French carpenter and chronicler André Pénicaut visited a Pascagoula village (in what is now Biloxi) where he and his travel companions received smoked meats of buffalo, bear, and deer along with melons, wild fruits, and sagamité. From the beginning of European occupation, the settlers relied heavily on Native American communities for food, drink, and shelter. This proto-exchange economy of immigrants trading guns and other European imports for Native foodstuffs marks the birth of Louisiana Creole cuisine.

This colonial space of social interaction and cultural change formed the foundation for Louisiana's increasingly diverse and growing society. The essence of the boucherie is turning flesh into meat or, dare I say, nature into culture. The acts of hunting, killing, processing, and consuming are cultural acts: they are expressions of ancestral lineage, environmental competency, intelligence, ethnic identity, and culinary skill and preferences. By killing, processing, and eating animals—natural, living things—people create, express, and consume their own culture. Whether the animal is a wild bear, deer, hog, or peccary, people make culture out of nature as soon as they choose to turn an animal into food.

According to John F. McDermott, sagamité was a commonly consumed corn-based dish consisting of hominy boiled in either salty water or tallow (usually from bears) and sometimes containing spices, beans, and other vegetables. It deserves its own book because of its rich history of linguistic errancy. Although the word is Algonquin, traveling south along with French speakers from northeast Canada, the dish (and the techniques used to make it) traveled northward as corn cultivation spread from Mexico throughout North America. Corn-based dishes like sagamité are often overlooked and underappreciated in the field of Louisiana studies and deserve more exploration.

Pigs and People

I focus in this book on the butchering of pigs (pork), but cows, sheep, poultry, and other fowl were also killed and processed in boucheries. When I was working as a butcher, I could not help but notice the predominance of pork products on the shelves; pork consumption has always been higher in the South than in other areas of the country. Unlike other farm animals such as cows and chickens, pigs were hunted and domesticated exclusively for their flesh. They were also relatively easy animals to raise. Semi-feral hogs were essentially self-sufficient in the spring, summer, and fall; they foraged in nearby woods for wild fruits, nuts, and berries and ate unharvested sweet potatoes, fruits, and vegetables left in the fields. To fatten them up, farmers would enclose the hogs in pens in the late fall and feed them only corn for several weeks. Whatever they ate, pigs converted this food to meat quickly and efficiently, at nearly six times the rate of cows and sheep.

In the northeastern colonies, Dutch settlers introduced the technique of salting their meat—primarily the shoulders and hams—and packing it in barrels for trade. Salted pork soon became one of these colonies' biggest exports. In Spanish Louisiana, most of the meat was supplied by Native hunting parties, but this supply needed to be supplemented by expensive imports from New England. In the 1770s, the Spanish government looked to strengthen Louisiana's meat industry by encouraging competition among the local meat markets. A primary contractor would lease butcher shops to local butchers, and competition between investors boosted the size of cattle and hog herds. By 1789, the government, according to John Folse and George Rodrigue, introduced a free-market system to the urban meat markets. There were standardized retail prices for beef and pork, and butchers rented stalls in markets located just outside city limits. Local herders and hunters, usually Native people, supplied the cattle and pigs to the butchers. At that time, bear fat remained an important staple in Louisiana cuisine but was sold in rendered form at the markets.

Pigs quickly became the preferred meat-based protein in Louisiana diets, and they were soon found wild and domesticated all over the American South. The feral razorbacks of the Southeast, the feral and semi-feral pigs of the Northeast salted pork trade, and many other varieties brought to the United States in the eighteenth and nineteenth centuries accompanied Europeans on their westward march; by the twentieth century, pigs were being hunted and domesticated in every continental state. In the South, pigs were the basis of many occasions for social interaction beginning in the early nineteenth century. Hog drives from fall to early winter in Alabama, East Tennessee, Georgia, and the Carolinas; pig roasts; festivals revolving around swine; and boucheries cemented the pig's place as a survival practice and economic staple. Our revitalization of these rituals makes them cultural symbols in the South alongside cotton and fiddle music.

The South's economy was crippled by the Civil War, and farmers had to rely on one or two cash crops to survive. As they poured more of their resources into these cash crops, they had to spend more money on store-bought supplies. The South had no choice but to adopt the rapid modernization and industrialization of the North. Grocery stores like the Piggly Wiggly chain (founded in 1916) profited from farmers no longer raising their own pigs and urban southerners' hunger for pork, and small restaurants came on the culinary scene in the early twentieth century. The South's attachment to pastoral culture came to be observed more and more in its foodways and other cultural expressions. Even if fewer people grew their own pigs, southerners satisfied their obsession with pork in other ways.

Pork culture knew no racial or class boundaries. Black- and white-owned barbecue restaurants dotted the American South, and Native American communities also benefited economically from the new industrialized pork economy. According to S. Jonathan Bass, the Choctaw Nation had already begun hosting annual boucheries and pig roasts in the late nineteenth century. At-home hog rituals, conversely, saw a decline in the early twentieth century. With precut, processed, and packaged meats available to southern farmers, the hog-killing ritual slowly gave way to livestock shows and contests. Judges scored pigs based on beauty, disposition, size, symmetry, health, and more. But pork's place in southern society has endured due to the region's appreciation of its gastronomic distinctiveness.

Among the countless ways to cook a pig, from 500 BC China to the twenty-first-century American South, barbecue has been the preferred method. Barbecue pork meat evolved from a holiday and special event dish to a staple in southern cuisine. Variations of barbecue style are closely tied to place. Different regions within the South boast their own styles and accompaniments to their own barbecue, as manifested in sauces, breads, sides, and cooking methods. The Louisiana boucherie and *cochon de lait* are Louisiana's offerings to the South's wide array of pork celebrations.

Despite the decline in hog husbandry, American farmers continued to raise pigs well into the twentieth century by either penning them and feeding them grain and scraps or allowing them to roam in the woods where they would feed themselves. Those in the woods were rounded up for slaughter usually in the fall, but some escaped to become feral hogs. They joined the many other feral hogs, such as the South's notorious razorbacks. Today, according to Mark Essig, there are more than five million feral swine in the United States.

Like the rest of the United States, Louisiana is home to feral hogs and all eight major breeds of domesticated pigs: Yorkshire (by far the largest breed in North America), Duroc, Berkshire, Hampshire, Poland China, Landrace, Spotted, and Chester White. According to the LSU College of Agriculture, there were more than eight thousand domesticated pigs in Louisiana in 2020, representing all eight major breeds, as well as crossbred or hybrids. Hybrid pigs make up 80 percent of the national commercial pork market. Louisiana's Department of Wildlife and Fisheries estimates that the state is home to more than 700,000 feral hogs, which can be found in all sixty-four parishes.

In Louisiana, Yorkshire, Berkshire, and Hampshire breeds are favored because they grow lean meat quickly and efficiently. This is a change from the early twentieth century when pigs with substantial amounts of fat, especially back fat, were preferred; much of that fat was used as lard or tallow for cooking oil, wax, soap, lamp oil, preservatives, and candles. After World War II, American consumers began preferring vegetable-based cooking oils to lard for health reasons, which led to pig breeders prioritizing leaner pigs with minimal back fat.

Many Louisianans revere local traditions surrounding pigs, and as a result, the boucherie is an event equally important today for cultural expression as it once was for communal survival. Ronald William Lewis, a retired streetcar track repairman born in New Orleans in 1951 and currently living and barbecuing in the city's Lower Ninth Ward, expresses his own connection to the south Louisiana foodscape this

With most of the work complete, butchers and participants gather to drink beer and play Cajun music at an annual family boucherie.

way: "My uncle who lived on a plantation all his life would kill a hog every fall. We would go out there early in the morning. They would gut him and clean him and disperse the meat. My mother would come back and make hog cracklings." The culinary influences of Black farmers, butchers, and cooks in Louisiana who shaped and molded the regional cuisine known as Creole food live today in the memories of Louisiana's butchers, pitmasters, chefs, eaters, and festivalgoers.

A Forgotten Little Africa

In her book *High on the Hog: A Culinary Journey from Africa to America,* Jessica Harris provides a compelling account of how African farmers and cooks quietly and seamlessly colonized the palates of white

Europeans in the American South beginning with the first arrival of the enslaved in 1719. Most of the enslaved were from the Senegambian region, which specialized in rice cultivation along the low-lying delta of the Gambia River. According to chef and cookbook author Michael Twitty, of the six thousand Africans brought to Louisiana between 1719 and 1731, four thousand were from the Upper Guinea coast and Senegal, which was home to the Wolof, Mandinka, Fula, Serer, Bamana, and Jola peoples. Each of these groups habitually hunted and consumed a wide array of wildlife inhabiting the natural prairies on and along the Senegal River. Beef, sheep, goats, and fowl—such as partridges, guinea fowl, wood pigeons, sea birds, and migratory birds—constituted a significant portion of the meat-based protein consumed by inhabitants of this region, as noted by historian Gwendolyn Midlo Hall.

At bustling towns like New Orleans and Natchitoches, Indigenous people, Africans, and Europeans gathered to exchange goods, usually food items, and in the process inevitably exchanged cultural knowledge, linguistic traits, and foodways. On any given day in mid-eighteenth-century south Louisiana, one might observe a Chitimacha woman trading a "deer(skin) of oil" to a European for a rifle or fabric. Or perhaps an enslaved African would be trading tobacco to an Ishak man for corn or French coins. Both Indigenous people and enslaved Africans contributed to the formation of Louisiana Creole cuisine.

Harris discusses the two most common ways in which enslaved Black workers received meals each day on southern plantations: either their food was prepared by fellow slaves in a centralized kitchen on the plantation, or they were supplied rations and allowed to prepare the food in their own cabins or within communities they created for themselves. The former system was more common in the early years of enslavement, when the enslaved workers were often housed in dormitories and lived communally. Distribution rations became more common as the enslaved population grew. In both scenarios, enslaved Blacks worked together to prepare their own food, engaging in culinary collaboration.

Even though Africans and Afro-Creoles dominated the kitchens of eighteenth- and nineteenth-century Louisiana, contemporary researchers must look deep into primary sources to discover the countless ways that Africans influenced Louisiana agriculture and cooking. In the 1930s, the Library of Congress launched the Works Progress Administration; in one of its major projects, formerly enslaved Blacks were interviewed about their lives in the antebellum South. These interviews provided invaluable insight into the conditions of slavery. In 1937, ninety-year-old Valmar Cormier (my own distant relative)—a bilingual (French and English) and biracial (born to a white father and Black mother) Creole and a formerly enslaved Black, then living in Lafayette, Louisiana—recalled eating raw snails found in the woods and using bits of pork fat from boucheries as bait to catch enough crawfish for a pot of gumbo. Like many enslaved Blacks, Cormier ingeniously diversified a monotonous diet by using some pork fat as bait to make a gumbo, thereby enhancing the nutritional value of the food he received. Earlier in this interview, Cormier described boucheries practiced while he was a child, saying "Dey'd kill de brutes and keep and save all de tallow and one day was set off to make de candles. All de neighbors come and dey have kind of party and eat and things. Sometime dey make three, four hunnerd candles in one day and lay dem in a big box, so dey won't get break. Us make soap on de plantation, too. Dey melt de tallow and cracklin's and git lye out de fireplace ash. We have cotton and corn and potatoes growin' so we has plenty to eat. Us have coosh-coosh, dat cornbread and meat."

This account of a boucherie is quite different from the description presented at the beginning of this chapter. Given his age at the time of the interview, Cormier was describing boucheries performed annually in or near Lafayette in the mid-nineteenth century. Interestingly, his description resembles more of a candle- and soap-making ritual than a culinary event. Of course, the pigs' meat was also being processed for consumption, but candles and soap evidently were important parts of the event. Thus, the boucherie transcended sustenance and produced a variety of forms of material culture. Indeed, tallow was used for lamps until after the turn of the twentieth century, and people in rural Louisiana were still making soap from tallow and homemade lye into the mid-twentieth century.

In the rest of the interview, Cormier emphasized the importance of starchy carbohydrates such as sweet potatoes and corn in his diet. He also mentioned cotton, which would have been used for clothing, bedding, and trade. He recalled eating couche-couche, a blend of cornmeal, milk, and salty pork that resembled, in name and appearance, couscous, which originated in North Africa. Though the name of this dish traveled to Louisiana with Africans, couche-couche was also similar to the Native American dish of corn grits mixed with liquid and chunks of meat, eaten hot or cold. The Choctaw word for this dish is Tanchi Lakchi, which refers to the method of drying whole-kernel hominy (known in Louisiana as *sagamité*), pounding it into grits using a mortar and pestle, and then boiling it with water and meat. When French people arrived in the Lower Mississippi Valley, they preferred adding milk to this mixture. Thus, the food that Cormier and thousands of other people were eating in nineteenth- and early twentieth-century Louisiana was a blend of Indigenous, African, and French foodways. Many Louisianans still eat couche-couche today.

Food writer Michael Twitty describes south Louisiana, east Texas, and the American South as "a forgotten Little Africa." From rice to rock n' roll, we can observe elements of the African Diaspora alongside other diasporas and cultures. Wherever Africans, African Americans, and Afro-Creoles found themselves in the South, despite the circumstances, they turned place into home. Therefore, along with a variety of ingredients and cooking techniques, agricultural know-how, and many other culinary skills, West Africans brought to the Americas a profound sense of empathy and hospitality. These virtues are represented in the food culture of the African Diaspora in America. The same gestures—welcoming strangers and visitors into the home with food and drink—that the Wolof call *teranga* and the Mandinka call *diorama,* those in Louisiana and the South simply call southern hospitality.

The Acadians

The first Acadians arrived in the New World in what is today Canada at the dawn of the seventeenth century. They shared subsistence lifeways with the Indigenous hunter-fisher-gatherer population for more than a century before their exile. Between November 1754 and

1764, approximately 11,500 (of a total population of 14,100) Acadians were deported to the thirteen British colonies in what would become the United States, as well as to the British Caribbean colonies, England, and France. This mass deportation would come to be known as "Le Grand Dérangement" or the "Great Upheaval." After years of cultural, linguistic, and economic marginalization and isolation in the Atlantic colonies of Saint-Domingue, Maryland, Pennsylvania, New York, and Nova Scotia, about one thousand Acadians boarded English merchant ships and sought refuge in Spanish Louisiana. At a cost of 200 pesos, its governor Antonio de Ulloa provided incoming Acadian families with six hens, one rooster, one cow either with calf or pregnant, 160 to 240 arpents of land (one arpent is slightly smaller than one acre), corn, gunpowder, bullets, and a musket.

However, Acadians were unhappy with their allotted land, considering it to be too far from the port and market of New Orleans. They resisted the Spanish governor's order that they settle in Louisiana's northeastern frontier settlement of Natchez, and so the first bands of Acadians moved to the east and west banks of the Mississippi River at Cabannocé, Côte des Allemands, and St. Gabriel. After an epidemic that occurred around the same time, other Acadians dispersed to the west, settling near present-day Breaux Bridge, Lafayette, and Opelousas. After Ulloa repeatedly threatened to separate and even deport Acadian families, many took part in the uprising of 1768 that ultimately ousted Louisiana's first Spanish governor. All the while, Acadians relied on their agricultural skills, their environmental adaptability, and the cohesiveness that had already helped them survive on the eastern Canadian frontier.

By the 1780s, land from the Vermilion River area to the Grand Prairie region northwest of present-day Lafayette was thickly populated with Acadian grantees, who could farm these plains with little land-clearing required. They interacted with equally tight-knit Indigenous communities such as the Opelousas, Ishak, and Chitimacha and learned from them how to thrive on the land where waterways met the prairie. Economic, environmental, and (over)population factors, as well as hostile Creole colonists, forced Acadian families to fan out to the south toward present-day Broussard, New Iberia, and Maurice and to the west to settle in Lewisburg, Church Point, and Faquetaique (southeast of present-day Eunice). Acadians continued immigrating to Louisiana into the nineteenth century, following rich waterways into resource-filled plains and forests and thriving in the relatively mild climate. They sought more and more isolated areas such as the lower Lafourche area, where many of their Francophone descendants live today.

Many Acadians found success as farmers, fishermen, tradesmen, and cattle drivers. In the fall, following the example of Louisiana Creoles, Indigenous groups, and others, Acadians slaughtered surplus hogs and cattle. They consumed some of the pork or beef immediately but preserved most of the meat by salting or smoking. They preferred salt pork over wild game, just as did the Acadians who remained in the Bay of Fundy area (between Nova Scotia and New Brunswick). Canadian boucheries took place in the harvest season and were means of preparing food to be eaten during the winter months. At the time of their expulsion from the Canadian Maritimes, soupe de la Toussaint—a turnip and cabbage soup that occasionally contained salt pork—was a staple in Acadian diets, which also included wheat, barley, rye, ground grains, and apples stored in cold cellars. Acadians mostly boiled or fried their meats and vegetables in black cast-iron cookware.

After they moved to Louisiana, the Acadians relied on Native American food practices for sustenance, such as frying meat and fish in bear oil. Farm families typically ate salt pork, cornbread, and seasonal vegetables and fruits such as tomatoes, cucumbers, corn, sweet potatoes, berries, peas, beans, peanuts, apples, bananas, pears, peaches, and more. Rice was rarely consumed except in years when the corn crop failed.

Shortly after their arrival in Louisiana, most Acadian farmers acquired one to three enslaved Black workers, and so Acadian foodways soon took on West African influences. They cultivated and consumed rice; used okra especially in gumbo, as seen in recipes for gumbo from the Acadian Coast as early as 1804; and cooked meat-based sauces (known today as gravies) made by frying meat and vegetables in oil, then adding water or broth, and sometimes thickening with roux. These meat-based gravies, which were occasionally served over rice or with corn, represent the cultural mosaic of Louisiana's colonial and American history. The Senegalese dish boeuf mafé—a beef stew with beef cubes smothered in cooking oil, bell peppers, chili peppers, onions, garlic, and sweet potatoes, thickened with peanut butter, and served over rice—exemplifies the strong African influence on Louisiana Acadian and Creole cuisine.

Many second- and third-generation Acadians embraced the institution of slavery along with Creole materialistic values, increasing the numbers of slaves they owned. However, some Acadians kept their farms small with just a few enslaved workers, whereas others were *petits habitants,* subsistence farmers without slaves. This latter group was displaced by the rise of Louisiana's plantation system in the early- to mid-nineteenth century. Most of these displaced Acadians moved to the lower Lafourche Valley or to St. Landry, Terrebonne, Assumption, and St. Mary Parishes. These prairie Acadians, like much of the South's poor white population in the nineteenth century, ate mostly corn and other vegetables grown at home, such as sweet potatoes and peas, dairy products, and occasionally pork.

Following the boom in the sugarcane industry in the early nineteenth century, many Acadians left the River Parishes for present-day Lafayette, St. Landry, Acadia, St. Martin, and Calcasieu Parishes, where they acquired more land and established *vacheries,* or cattle ranches. By 1850, 25 percent of Acadian ranches in Calcasieu Parish boasted more than five hundred head of beef cattle, and only 2 of the 233 Acadian households in southwestern Louisiana lacked horses. Acadian ranchers relied heavily on Creole horses and beef cattle for income and on other livestock such as hogs and chickens to supplement their flexitarian diet.

Travelogues written by visitors to antebellum Louisiana indicate that the families of *petits habitants* relied on homegrown vegetables, beans, peas, fruits, and nuts. They ate lots of eggs, salt pork, and wild game. During the annual *ramasserie* (communal harvest), they harvested corn, Irish potatoes, sweet potatoes, peas, beans, pumpkins, okra, and, in times of heavy rain, rice. Acadians were also known to have grown peaches, figs, oranges, pecans, raisins, grapes, and quinces. Meat—beef, poultry, and pork—was typically eaten fresh in the summer.

Semi-domesticated grass-fed longhorn cattle, wild game, and old chickens that no longer produced eggs yielded tough meat that required lengthy cooking for tenderization. Thus, we observe the development of soups, stews, gravies, and sauces that reflected the creolization of antebellum Louisiana foodways. For example, during a boucherie, one participant might have prepared a stew using meat from the pig's backbone, a less fatty cut of meat than that of the front- or hindquarters. The meat would be fried in rendered hog lard—as the Choctaw would have done using bear fat and wild game meat—before adding water and boiling the meat for a long time to create a gravy and tenderize it; this was reminiscent of the Senegalese stewing method discussed earlier. Therefore, the all-important method of braising meat to make a gravy is an amalgamation of Native American, West African, and French/French-Acadian foodways. This dish would have been eaten as is or perhaps with cornbread, rice, or potatoes. Acadian farmers from the lower Lafourche area also boiled saltwater shellfish to eat plain or in gumbo. Boudin required the boiling and then grinding of meat, fat, and entrails; mixing with blood, rice, and spices; and stuffing into intestines that served as casing. Hog's head cheese was made by boiling the pig's head—and often the feet—until the collagen formed a gelatinous mixture. This gelatin was then mixed with cheek meat and other edible material taken from the head, salted, and allowed to cool.

Frying pans and Dutch ovens were scarce in nineteenth-century Louisiana, so people primarily cooked in kettles and other cast-iron cookware over an open flame. Acadians who did own frying pans used them primarily to bake cornbread and fry couche-couche. Although corn flour was the primary agent for bread making west of the Atchafalaya Basin, for Acadians living east of there, wheat flour was much more accessible—so they baked bread in outdoor, dome-shaped ovens and wheat was a more important component in their diet.

Just downriver from the Acadian Coast was the Côte des Allemands, or German Coast. By 1752, this area was home to approximately 250 German settlers. Like all the other immigrant groups in the Lower Mississippi Valley, Germans brought with them a rich and influential knowledge of agriculture and cooking. Before long, these influences manifested along the Mississippi River and spread westward. German-designed barns dotted the central prairies; smokehouses converted from chicken coops and potato curing houses were used to smoke sausages, andouille, stomachs, and more; and German diatonic accordions were played at house parties called fais do-do and at boucheries. In the German prairie settlement of Robert's Cove in south-central Louisiana, oral tradition indicates that German settlers ate bratwurst—a pork-based sausage—and other traditionally German foods.

More Germans immigrated to Louisiana between 1820 and 1850 after the Napoleonic Wars, making them the third-largest linguistic group in Louisiana behind the French and Spanish. Like Acadians, they worked on plantations and in New Orleans as farmers, builders, and blacksmiths. The last wave of German immigration came near the end of the nineteenth century. Like the immigrants before them from Alsace, Lorraine, Palatinate, Württemberg, Strasbourg, Baden, Bavaria, and Augsburg, these immigrants imported their own foodways, which were from southern Germany. Their diet included roasted beef, dairy products, wine, beer, cabbages, smoked sausages, and seven-herb soup—made with mustard greens, collards, turnip tops, beet tops, parsley, spinach, and purslane and flavored with salt pork—similar to today's *gumbo z'herbes,* or green gumbo. Although the German language has all but disappeared from the region, their impact on Louisiana Creole cuisine remains evident in the smoked pork products found in nearly every contemporary representation of "Cajun food."

Much of what is often called "Acadian cuisine" and later "Cajun cuisine" is essentially a creolized cuisine that developed long before the arrival of Acadians to Louisiana. As Acadians spread out across south Louisiana, they took on the agricultural practices, values, and culinary techniques of the Creole and Indigenous communities. They also used ingredients indigenous to Louisiana, as well as those brought to Louisiana by Indigenous peoples, West Africans, the French, the Spanish, and other immigrants. They intermarried with Indigenous and Creole communities, as well as nineteenth-century German, Italian, and English immigrants to Louisiana.

The foodscape in which Acadians lived influenced their own way of cooking much more than the reverse. Yet, Acadians did have an impact on Louisiana Creole cuisine, as can be seen by the evolution of Acadian cuisine in the state. There are several parallels between the two regional cuisines. In *Pantry and Palate: Remembering and Rediscovering Acadian Food,* Simon Thibault describes traditional

Acadian pork dishes like fromage à la tête de cochon or hog's head cheese and boudin. Acadian and Creole cuisines both reflect an appreciation for the entire animal being slaughtered, in this case the pig. Up until the early twentieth century, both cuisines used every part of the animal. Acadians in both French Canada and Louisiana killed pigs for their meat and rendered the fats for soap, candles, and cooking oil. They salted much of the meat and used the entrails for boudin and other sausages. It is important to note that boudin was eaten in French Canada and is one of numerous pork products imported by French immigrants to the Americas, along with andouille, salted pork, smoked sausage, and hog's head cheese; these are Europe's primary contributions to the Louisiana boucherie, either directly to the Lower Mississippi Valley via the Caribbean and French Canada, or by other means. However, boudin was being made by North American Indigenous people long before the arrival of any of these other groups; it consisted of buffalo meat, fat, and kidney suet stuffed into buffalo intestines and fried in bear fat. The Native people served it to early French colonists who, in travel journals like Henri Joutel's *Journal of LaSalle's Last Voyage,* described it as boudin.

Each culture represented throughout Louisiana's rich history of immigration engaged in communal efforts to survive, and the traditions that spring from these efforts are especially vibrant in the fall. This sense of community was strengthened by *ramasseries* and boucheries. Acadians worked together to survive the frigid Canadian Maritimes, mass deportation, exile, and semi-tropical Louisiana. They sought upward mobility in capitalist America and were melded into Louisiana's cultural and culinary melting pot. They were white, they bought enslaved Blacks, and they situated themselves within the complicated racial stratification. They ultimately became Louisiana's most well-known ethnic group in the mid- to late twentieth century through a phenomenon called "Cajunization," which I explore in the next chapter by examining my favorite form of literature: cookbooks.

3

How Cajun Is the Boucherie?

Invariably, an internet search for information on Louisiana food and cookbooks first delivers websites on Cajun and Creole cuisines, the former being much more prominent. The search for "best Louisiana cookbooks" will provide links to articles such as "Top 10 Cajun Cookbooks" and "86 Best Cajun Cooking Books of All Time." And googling "Louisiana creole cookbooks" will produce books from well-known, self-proclaimed Cajun chefs such as *Chef Paul Prudhomme's Louisiana Kitchen* (1984) by Paul Prudhomme, *The Encyclopedia of Cajun & Creole Cuisine* (2004) by John D. Folse, and *Mosquito Supper Club: Cajun Recipes from a Disappearing Bayou* (2020) by Melissa M. Martin. Some notable cookbooks that discuss the *boucherie* are *Chasing the Gator: Isaac Toups and the New Cajun Cooking* (2018) by Isaac Toups and *Cajun Pig: Boucheries, Cochon de Laits and Boudin* (2020) by Dixie Poché.

To learn more about the origins of the boucherie, I analyzed twenty-six cookbooks published between 1885 and 2021. Cookbooks allow readers to purchase access to Louisiana food culture and re-create its edible cultural elements; they give insiders a platform on which they can construct and express their own cultural identity; and they ultimately serve as a medium for recording memories, experiences, recipes, attitudes, and values regarding the cuisine and culture in question. Melissa Martin, in *Mosquito Supper Club,* sums up well the importance of cookbooks: "Food (and eating it) is our common denominator, and all ingredients have a story."

In deciding which cookbooks to study, I prioritized twenty-six that were published either under the Cajun or Creole label and that mentioned the boucherie, pork, or both. I mostly focus on Cajun cookbooks published in the 1980s and 1990s, especially those written by chefs Paul Prudhomme and John Folse. Authors of published cookbooks—like Prudhomme and Folse—package and export culture in a way that can be commodified and hold monetary value. I show how these cookbooks contribute to the understanding and misunderstanding of the boucherie.

Louisiana Becomes a Cajun Foodscape

In *The Cajuns: Americanization of a People,* Shane Bernard writes, "Cookbooks played a major role in commercializing Cajun culture and introducing it to the rest of America." He asserts that the earliest mention of Cajun food was in *Creole Cajun Cookery,* a cookbook published annually by the *Daily Iberian* newspaper beginning in 1952. Like many other micro-ethnic movements inspired by the civil rights movements that swept the nation in the 1960s, newfound Cajun pride led to the rapid exportation of Cajun culture in the 1970s and 1980s. This period saw a resurgence of Cajun music and the embracing of French immersion programs in public schools spearheaded by Jimmy Domengeaux, former director of the Council for the Development of French in Louisiana. Congrès Mondial Acadien, a celebration that reunited south Louisianans with distant relatives in French Canada, also contributed to the discovery and embrace of Cajun culture by Cajuns and non-Cajuns. The culinary surge that began in the 1980s introduced the nation to Louisiana's unique foodways, but it also led to a rise of faux Cajun products in grocery stores and restaurants. The misrepresentation of Cajuns as backward swamp dwellers on television and in cinema also helped heighten America's infatuation with Cajun culture, which increased tourism in Acadiana but disrupted folk rituals.

Cookbooks were one of the main means through which Cajuns defined their own culture and simultaneously allowed outsiders to purchase access to this exoticized foodscape. Cajun chefs/writers used dishes created primarily by Black and Native cooks to define and export their culture. Figures like Prudhomme and Folse walked the line between exotic and white America as they wrote about and disseminated south Louisiana's collective memory, history, and recipes in cookbooks; unfortunately, by doing so they undermined the deep contributions of people of color presented in the previous chapter. Ultimately, through cultural preservation efforts, white Cajuns placed themselves at the center of Louisiana's ethnic mosaic by wielding discursive power in the region, controlling the cultural knowledge, appropriating Black and Indigenous foods, and claiming the boucherie and other elements of Louisiana food as their own.

One individual can be credited with kicking off the worldwide Cajun culinary craze that began in the early 1980s and continues still today—Cajun chef Paul Prudhomme. Drawing on his humble upbringing in Opelousas, Prudhomme brought culinary ingenuity and improvisation to his New Orleans restaurant, K-Paul's Louisiana Kitchen. Lacking the funds for a commercial grill, he experimented with a superheated iron skillet on which he created his famous blackened redfish. The dish became so popular that the redfish was nearly cooked into extinction. In response, the US Department of Commerce banned commercial fishing of redfish in 1986, and in the following year, recreational fishing of it was also prohibited.

Paul Prudhomme's cooking and persona became so popular that he took his kitchen on the road, setting up eateries in San Francisco and New York City. His cookbook, *Paul Prudhomme's Louisiana Kitchen* (1984), sold a half-million copies and appeared on the *New York Times* bestseller list for thirteen weeks. Prudhomme would go on to pen nine more cookbooks between 1984 and 2007, but none of them outsold his first, the book that introduced Cajun cooking to the world.

Paul Prudhomme begins his monumental cookbook by writing, "When the taste changes with every bite and the last bite is as good as the first, that's Cajun! I'm a Cajun and that's Louisiana cooking." Through this definition of Cajun cooking and his own ethnic and cultural identity, he immediately equates Cajun cooking with Louisiana cooking. He then goes on to provide a brief history of Cajuns, writing that they "originated in Southern France, emigrated to Nova Scotia in the early 1600's and settled a colony that came to be called Acadia." In one short paragraph, the author tells the story of the Cajuns coming from France to Acadia; being exiled from Acadia; immigrating to Louisiana where they settled along waterways to fish, trap, and farm; and culminating in the settling of the descendants of two of his ancestors near Opelousas, where he was born.

Like many south Louisianans born in the 1940s, Prudhomme was one of many siblings and the child of a sharecropper. He grew up helping his family on its farm, hence the appreciation of food and fresh ingredients found throughout this book. Prudhomme assures the novice reader, "The book is a teaching tool as well as a recipe book," and "the chapters are organized with the easiest [recipes] at the beginning." *Louisiana Kitchen* is therefore intended to be didactic and is written with non-Louisianans in mind. He insists that, by reading cookbooks and drawing on experiences or memories, anyone can cook. Although he recognizes that cooking is personal, and therefore no two dishes are alike, he tries to package and export Cajun cuisine in a way that is accessible, purchasable, and replicable.

It is important to note that Prudhomme's first cookbook does not directly mention the boucherie. In his next book, however, *The Prudhomme Family Cookbook: Old-Time Louisiana Recipes* (1987), the boucherie plays a central role. Here, Prudhomme takes a more personal approach to cookbook writing. He dives deeper into his childhood, personalizing his cooking style and perceptions of food. In *Louisiana Kitchen,* he sought to introduce the nation to Louisiana's cuisine(s), whereas *The Prudhomme Family Cookbook* provides insight into his own childhood and the family memories that molded him into the cook he would become.

Prudhomme recalls his father saying that, although the family did not have much, they had plenty to eat (in my collection of short stories, *Mal,* the grandfather figure boasts of a similar meat-based wealth in the chapter titled "Big Shots"). Prudhomme admits that before he was born in 1940 his family was very poor, and there was often "no meat for days because there weren't enough chickens to kill and there was no meat left from the last butchering." Although many cookbooks in this chapter discuss the abundance of meat provided by boucheries, Prudhomme invites the reader to recall the stark reality of being poor in 1930s and 1940s rural America: many people lived without adequate sustenance, even those surrounded by food crops. After World War II, many sharecroppers in Louisiana, like the Prudhomme family, were able to provide for their (usually large) families and, even though they often lacked enough money to keep up with the Joneses—by buying automobiles, new clothes, and agricultural machinery—they could produce enough food to live comfortably. Still, Prudhomme recalls his mother's exceptional ability to maximize food output: "No one could stretch food like my mom: she could take one old hen and a little bit of Cajun andouille sausage and make an incredible gumbo." By using andouille—a rich, energy-packed product of the boucherie—and gumbo, a water-based stew, Prudhomme's mother could feed many people with little food.

Prudhomme attributes andouille directly to Cajun cuisine, and because he was the only person writing about Louisiana cuisine at the time, what he wrote was taken as definitive. By claiming cultural ownership of andouille and other important boucherie ingredients, Prudhomme presents the boucherie, and its products, as a Cajun practice. He goes on to say that his family's abundant food supply made them "like rich people," because they had more than one hundred chickens, dozens of hogs, and many cows, calves, and horses. His family eventually sold their farm and used the money to buy a grocery store, where Prudhomme worked as a butcher and a cook.

This economic capital, in the form of sustenance and then funds, would provide Prudhomme with the means and culinary knowledge to become the most influential chef in Louisiana in the 1980s and into the 1990s. Through his promotion of Cajun cuisine, Prudhomme contributed to the upward mobility of Cajuns in Louisiana's social hierarchy. Yet even though many Cajuns indeed participated in boucheries and cooked with its products, such as andouille sausage, smoked panse (stuffed pig stomach), and salted pork, it was incorrect to assert that the boucherie and all that comes from it are strictly Cajun. As discussed in chapter 2, many rural Louisiana Creoles (Blacks and whites of French descent with no Acadian heritage), Anglo-Americans, German Louisianans, Francophone Indigenous groups, and others were practicing boucheries and eating meals like the ones found throughout Prudhomme's book.

Prudhomme goes on to describe his and his wife's goals when opening K-Paul's Louisiana Kitchen, when he was forced to pivot away from what he calls "Cajun food" to make it more suited to his customers' tastes and to be more restaurant-friendly. For example, he cooked with butter instead of lard, made sauces from stock rather than cooking one sauce throughout the entire day, and cooked meals to order instead of serving from one big pot. Prudhomme admits that "what [he] did in New Orleans changed the food—in some cases making it better, and in some, just changing it." This admission implies that Prudhomme chose to sacrifice authenticity for financial and social gain. Thus, his first cookbook *Louisiana Kitchen* "did not cover the old Cajun methods of cooking" but instead included adapted recipes from his restaurant.

That is why he had to write a second cookbook. In its introduction, he writes, "*The Prudhomme Family Cookbook* fulfills my desire to have a book that lets people see the way Cajun food originally was." Prudhomme is thus insisting that the recipes found in this book represent Cajun food, Cajun history, and Cajuns' environmental and economic competency and ingenuity. Furthermore, the word "originally," in this context, puts "Cajun" at the center. Prudhomme, a Cajun, claims ownership of the recipes that follow on behalf of his cultural group. He continues by listing ingredients that his family grew and meals that his family members liked to make. He oscillates between his family and Cajuns at large—the personal "we" and the collective "we"—thereby depicting his family as representative of all Cajuns. Furthermore, his being so well known and widely read paints Cajun as the central, dominant cuisine and cultural group of Louisiana, a notion that would only grow stronger in the following decades.

In *The Prudhomme Family Cookbook,* Prudhomme dives deeper into his rural upbringing and describes terms like *boucherie* and some of its elements and products in the section titled "Glossary & Notes from Our Test Kitchen." Thus, the boucherie, a ritual that is no longer practiced out of necessity, remains present in cookbooks. This presence in the cookbook medium begins with Prudhomme, who uses his writings to teach the world about the boucherie:

> Boucherie literally means butchering—but in Louisiana it means a festive, communal gathering at which several hogs and a steer are killed and the meat is dressed out and prepared for curing or refrigerating. There is always a wonderful feast featuring fresh pork and all the trimmings—potato salad, candied yams, gumbo, and lots of desserts. Boucheries can last for several days and they're always held in midwinter when it is quite cold. Most of the work of the boucherie is done outdoors so the meat can be kept cold. Pronounced *boo*-shuh-*ree.*

This passage describes Prudhomme's childhood boucherie. He defines the practice in a way that lets readers simultaneously learn about his upbringing and the sourcing, history, and culture of what was eaten. They can also come to understand the important ritual that produces the meals they may soon re-create. This definition provides social context for the recipes to come. Stories, narratives, personalization, and social context would remain constant and crucial elements in Louisiana cookbooks through the turn of the twenty-first century.

Prudhomme defines other "Cajun" ingredients and meals alongside his description of the boucherie, such as andouille—"the most popular Cajun smoked pure pork sausage. Pronounced ahn-*doo*-ee"—and boudin, a "Cajun sausage with rice mixed into the stuffing. The most popular type is white boudin, made with pork and usually just referred to as boudin; if pork blood is added, it becomes red boudin. Several other meats or seafood can also be used. Pronounced *boo*-dan, with only a hint of the 'n' on the end." Both products, according to Prudhomme, are Cajun, but, as we have seen, they are not exclusively Cajun. There is evidence of Indigenous inhabitants of the Lower Mississippi Valley making sausage described by French explorers as "boudin" in the late seventeenth century.

In defining the term *boucherie* here, Prudhomme implies that *boucherie* is a Cajun word. In his definition of "Cajun French," he writes, "We've done our best to spell correctly all Cajun words and phrases that we've used. . . . Cajun French has never been considered a written language. Rather, it is a spoken language that began taking on its own flavor and rules of usage as soon as the speakers left southern France." As mentioned before, the cookbook medium is inherently didactic and therefore communicative. Through its recipes, historical and social context, analyses, definitions, and style, it communicates more than just how to cook. The medium invites readers to participate in the contribution to and understanding of the cuisine and culture in question.

Indeed, Prudhomme intends to go beyond teaching readers how to cook: he also provides a lesson in sociolinguistics. This language lesson becomes interactive when Prudhomme writes, "Since Cajun French was rarely written, spelling and grammatical inflections important in a written language were simply not a consideration. We'd love your input, especially if you consider yourself of Cajun descent, on how the terms we use for foods and folkways may differ from what you know. Let us hear from you!" Here Prudhomme directly invites the readers, especially those within the Cajun culture, to provide input and feedback on his cookbook's presentation of Louisiana French; this communicates that he is not imposing his own definitions on readers nor attempting to cross any boundaries. Prudhomme uses his cookbook as a space not only to capture fleeting orally transmitted recipes but also to write down the language through which these recipes have long been conveyed.

In the 1970s and 1980s, Prudhomme offered a parallel way to participate in the Cajun ethnic revival via the cookbook medium. Therefore, the word *boucherie* and other French culinary terms like *boudin, gratons, andouille, paunce, bourrée, gombo,* and *filé* make their way into Prudhomme's text, because he values the language through which the cuisine has evolved. Like the cuisine that he is presenting, Prudhomme also claims the language as Cajun. He presents the dialect of French not as Louisiana French, but as Cajun French. Therefore, *boucherie* becomes a Cajun word, implying that it, the signifier, and all that it signifies are Cajun. Other important culinary signifiers such as *grillades, ti' sale,* and hog's head cheese become consequentially Cajun and simultaneously legitimized through their attachment to southern France, according to Prudhomme's contextual framework. The glossary of Cajun terms claims these signifiers as Cajun, so the cuisine that they describe becomes Cajun as well. These ingredients, recipes, and stories construct a personal memory that becomes collective as it is packaged and sold as representative of the Cajun identity. Cajun—more specifically, Prudhomme's representation of Cajun—therefore, becomes the emblematic Louisiana cuisine.

Each of Prudhomme's recipes is preceded by a story that provides both a personal and cultural context. Virtually every recipe has the

French name underneath the English. The stylistic choice to put English first and French underneath it is done for marketing purposes. Prudhomme is looking to sell his book to a national Anglophone readership. If he was interested only in preserving Cajun French, he would have put French first. In contrast, contemporary literature promoting Louisiana French, such as *Ô Malheureuse* (2019), edited by Ashlee Wilson Michot, provides poems in Louisiana French first, with English translations at the end of the book in a smaller font.

In many recipes, especially those using pork, Prudhomme emphasizes the importance of using fresh ingredients, particularly fresh meat, because all these recipes came from a time when people grew and raised their own food. He uses this content to enhance the personalization and romanticization of the boucherie. He introduces a recipe for *grillades,* for example, by writing,

> Six hogs might be killed to provide fresh meat for several weeks and to prepare enough smoked, cured, and canned meats to last for many months. Most of the meat was smoked or cured, but Mom and Dad Prudhomme canned very lean strips of pork, which they called "grillades" (pronounced gree-yahds). . . . The meat was cut from the bones and the bones with any remaining meat and fat went to make salt meat or Ti Sale. The family cooked the grillades outdoors in a huge cast-iron pot over a wood fire, stirring the meat with a clean shovel.

These contextual introductions serve as an autobiographical portion of the cookbook. Prudhomme legitimizes his connection to this style of cooking and foodways by inviting the reader to understand his rural childhood by seeing, smelling, hearing, and tasting the farm on which he was raised. He also aims to transmit food knowledge to future generations: a recurring theme in media promoting Cajun culture. The cookbook becomes a window through which readers might gain access to Cajun foodways, thereby solidifying the culture as authentic and important. The boucherie imagery contributes not only to contextualizing the recipes but, more importantly, also to legitimizing Prudhomme as an ambassador for Cajun cuisine. The romanticization of the boucherie legitimizes Cajun cuisine by giving it written origins, a language, and a story.

After more than a decade of commercial success and national fame, Prudhomme returned to the family values that he expounded on in *The Prudhomme Family Cookbook.* In his third cookbook, *Chef Paul Prudhomme's Louisiana Tastes,* published in 2000, he responds to the Americanization of the family—rather than contributing to it—and invites readers to use food and literature to instill traditional values in their own families. In the introduction, he laments the widespread fracturing of families: "I think there must be some connection between the loss of the daily family meal and the fracturing of families and their traditional values. I think that, as a nation, we're nearing a crisis with our children because many of them don't know who they are or what their heritage is." Prudhomme regrets the erosion of the Cajun culture he pridefully represented and disseminated throughout his career. His intention for this book is that readers will use it to cook delicious food in the hopes that cooking at home—instead of dining out—will help modern families fulfill Prudhomme's romanticized vision of preparing and then eating food together. He reminds readers that, just as his family used to collaborate on boucheries and other labor-intensive agricultural and culinary practices, they can invite family members to contribute to meal preparation—even though that is no longer necessary for sustenance—because food, in a social and cultural context, transcends survival. Prudhomme concludes his introduction this way: "As wonderful as it is for a family to eat together, it's even better when family members cook together! . . . Turn off the television, for you'll have a lot more fun talking and laughing as you cook. Before you know it, you'll have a wonderful dinner and a closer family."

Perhaps these words reflect Prudhomme's regrets about the Americanization of his Cajun people and the commodification of Cajun cuisine to which he directly contributed. Through his cookbooks, cooking shows, and food products, Prudhomme initiated a culinary movement that packaged and exported Cajun cuisine. The same family and communal values that Prudhomme touched on when discussing the boucherie and other culinary practices in his early works—adding words like "traditional" and "authentic" to ensure readers that they were buying access to Louisiana culture—became, in his later works, the values that he would rely on to de-Americanize America, the melting pot in which he feared Cajun culture was rapidly dissolving. The commercial power of the boucherie and its many elements brought Prudhomme and other Cajun chefs economic and cultural capital in the 1980s, which contributed to the preservation of Cajun as the proverbial cuisine and culture of Louisiana today.

The 1980s witnessed the emergence of another remarkable Louisiana chef and champion of Cajun cuisine, John D. Folse, who published *The Evolution of Cajun & Creole Cuisine* in 1989. While building on Prudhomme's national and global presence, Folse's approach to presenting Louisiana cuisine to his readership was different, beginning with the title of this cookbook. It makes two important points: Louisiana cuisine is plural and constantly evolving.

Folse presents a more contemporary contextualization of Louisiana cuisine. Though he does draw from historical content, he relies less on nostalgia than Prudhomme. Folse uses the gumbo as a symbol of influences from French, German, Caribbean, Native American, and West African cuisines. He recognizes the West African impact on Creole cuisine, as well as that of French culinary techniques, both in the home and in professional kitchens. Thus, Folse does not distinguish between Cajun and Creole cuisines, neither racially nor spatially. Through the cookbook medium, he presents his recipes as embedded in notions of creolization, sharing, and perpetual evolution.

However, his wording is, at times, problematic. For example, Haitian cuisine is the only cuisine described as "exotic," which implies that other cuisines are familiar, native to Louisiana, and conventional. Another disputable point is his implication that relations between European colonizers and Indigenous peoples were friendly. Such a notion ignores centuries of violence, exploitation, genocide, and erasure. However, Folse does recognize the contributions of Choctaw, Chitimacha, Houma, and other Indigenous cooks and butchers to the development of Louisiana cuisine via their use of native ingredients and cooking techniques.

It seems that Cajuns are the ones most interested in distinguishing themselves from Creoles; from an outsider's point of view, the two labels may seem interchangeable. In "The Cajunization of French Louisiana: Forging a Regional Identity," Canadian scholar Cécyle Trépanier reminds us that "the farther one stands from the reality and intricacy of community living, the easier it is to see French Louisiana as a cultural monolith."

Overall, Folse is moving the discourse surrounding Louisiana cuisine in a more accurate, research-based direction. He uses the cookbook medium to present the diversity and fluidity of Louisiana cuisine and a culinary lens to understand Louisiana's past. Yet even though he aims to present Louisiana as having multiple foodscapes, he—a white, affluent chef—inevitably perpetuates the myth that Cajun cuisine and all its ingredients, techniques, and rituals define Louisiana cuisine and that it is *primarily* the result of white European influence. Folse does acknowledge the important impact of Native American cooking techniques and food-sourcing abilities on Cajun cuisine, defining it as being "characterized by the use of wild game, seafoods, wild vegetation and herbs. From their association with the Indians, the Cajuns learned techniques to best utilize the local products from the swamps, bayous, lakes, rivers and woods. Truly remarkable are the variations that have resulted from similar ingredients carefully combined in the black iron pots of the Cajuns." Yet this statement still places Cajun culture at the center; other contributing groups, such as Indigenous groups, remain at the margins.

Folse continues his definition of Cajun cuisine by calling it a "'table in the wilderness,' a creative adaptation of indigenous Louisiana foods. It is a cuisine forged out of a land that opened its arms to a weary traveler, the Acadian." The paradoxical image of a table in the wilderness implies that Acadians (and Europeans) brought their table—a symbol of civilization—to the wild foodscape of an Indigenous land. This image paints white Europeans as the main characters in the Louisiana story. Yet, without Indigenous food knowledge and sourcing, Europeans would not have survived that wilderness.

Folse's words are powerful: he uses cookbook content to legitimize his own perspective. Like Prudhomme, Folse is a proud Cajun. Through culinary discourse, he exports Cajun culture as being representative of Louisiana culture. The word *Cajun* comes to represent the region's constantly evolving creolized culture.

His memories, experiences, and success reinforce the notion of authenticity in his texts. His descriptions of the boucherie are remarkably like those of Prudhomme; they are full of powerful images as he sets the scene: "The men began to arrive before dawn to light the fires and kill the hogs. The children slept as the mules were hitched and awaited that moment when a nudge and a pat would hoist the hogs over the branch of an oak tree and onto the tables for cleaning."

Over the years, cookbooks have contributed to a larger effort within the culture to preserve records of the boucherie. Cookbooks like Folse's, however, only contribute to the storying of the event. The pastoral imagery of farmers waking before dawn to perform the ritual sets the event in a romanticized past. The reproduction of this version of the boucherie in the form of storytelling creates a kind of mythological boucherie. This repetition and continuity in Cajun media reinforce the idea that the boucherie is a Cajun ritual. The two principal Cajun chefs and food writers of the era confirm what the butchering ritual is and who practices it. Therefore, all the sauces, sausages, and recipes that come from the boucherie are ostensibly Cajun too. Readers must accept their words as authentic because they have no other perspective to compare this cuisine to. Folse and Prudhomme use memory and status to establish their Cajun cuisine as the main representative of Louisiana cuisine.

Folse concludes his reminiscence of the boucherie with these words: "It was late in the evening when the weary butchers made their way home with a child in one arm and the bounty of the boucherie in the other. Tired from their work, they were full of stories and gossip but refreshed by the dancing and sounds of laughter which faded into the night." The description offers an idyllic view of Francophone Louisiana. Such romanticized descriptions anchor the ritual in the past and imply an authentic original model to be preserved through repetition. The boucherie is presented as a ritual that invites readers and spectators to recognize community values, family ties, hard work, environmental competence, and the notion that meat eaters must take life to sustain life.

Another glaring element of these representations of the boucherie is the lack of women. The butchering ritual is presented as a male-dominated practice: men are the butchers and cooks. Women are pushed to the margins as eaters at best. The boucherie as a mythicized ritual is therefore used to marginalize virtually all members of Louisiana's cultural groups who are not white Cajun men. Just as the boucherie is used in some of these texts as a tool to divide and marginalize, it can also be used to blur lines and encourage inclusivity. In Folse's work, the boucherie is used to accomplish both. It simultaneously marginalizes women and people of color by leaving them out of the narrative, solidifying their lower position in ethnic, gender, and cultural hierarchies, and it is also used as a space to recognize more of the plurality of influences on Louisiana cuisine than Prudhomme's version of the story.

The Boucherie in Twenty-First-Century Cookbooks

The twenty-first-century canon of Louisiana cookbooks shifts the discourse surrounding Cajun and Creole cuisines, yet the commercialization of mainstream Louisiana cuisine and the Cajun name is still strong. Although memory continues to play a role in defining Louisiana's culinary mosaic, the personal and collective past are mobilized to create a more coherent view of contemporary Louisiana cuisine. Some contemporary chefs dive deeper into their own past, question the collective understanding of Louisiana cooking, debunk myths, correct misconceptions, and present new perspectives on the history and state of Louisiana cooking.

Cookbooks are and have always been a visually and textually fragmented form of literature. Recipes are organized as lists of ingredients and of didactic instructions, with varying amounts of space left for interpretation and creative freedom. Often, cookbooks do not offer recipes for complete meals, instead offering short prose descriptions and photos. They act as a medium of communication between one kitchen and another, between the experiences of one cook and many others, between eaters. After buying or downloading the cookbook, readers must continue to actively participate in the exchange. They can prepare, store, and eat meals and are invited to contribute to the narrativization of the cuisine in question. Readers are also encouraged to consider their own perceptions and misconceptions of that culture. Contemporary cookbook writers push the fragmentary form further to invite the reader to fill in the blanks with their own take on cooking and their own memories, experiences, and expectations. They use the cookbook as a fragmentary form and the boucherie as a tool to question the Louisiana cuisine that exists in the collective memory and to present a new, more coherent look at the cuisine.

In *Real Cajun: Rustic Home Cooking from Donald Link's Louisiana: A Cookbook* (2009), Donald Link—chef and owner of several New Orleans restaurants including Herbsaint, Pêche Seafood Grill, and Cochon Butcher—offers a more contemporary chef's take on Cajun cuisine as part of the larger complex foodscape of New Orleans. For Link, food is inseparable from place. What he calls Cajun food is a consumable, artistic representation of Louisiana as a landscape and foodscape. Link creates food as a way of preserving the threatened culture and geography of Louisiana. He asserts that recipes—when written or cooked—can be useful in capturing and celebrating a place. In *Real Cajun,* he presents the community of Acadia Parish in its culinary context to evoke his own sense of that place. He writes narratives and recipes drawn from his own memory to give life to the foodscape of his childhood in cookbook form. Link claims that the food he cooks is "typical of Acadia Parish," a historically Franco-Acadian parish in central Louisiana. Link, therefore, does not claim that all Louisiana cuisine is Cajun.

Link goes on to define Cajun food (of Acadia Parish) by providing a history of the area. He asserts that south Louisiana, as a landscape and a foodscape, is "incredibly diverse"; "Acadia Parish was settled by French exiles from Canada" and was also a destination for many German immigrants. Although Link tells his version of Louisiana food history through an Acadian-centric lens, he makes one simple yet major change to the approach used in the works of Prudhomme and Folse: Link employs the pronoun "I" and rarely the collective "we." It seems as if Link overtly intends to correct the misinformation provided by his predecessors. He refers directly to Prudhomme's inaccuracies when he writes, "This kind of cooking may or may not sound familiar to you, so before we go any further let's get one thing straight: The overly spiced and blackened food that gained popularity in the 1970s is nothing like the authentic Cajun food that I grew up with."

Link's cooking is strongly tied to personal memory. His childhood forms the foundation for his personal notion of "authenticity." Because he identifies as Cajun, real Cajun food or "authentic Cajun food" is what he ate and observed other Cajuns eating throughout his life in Cajun Louisiana. Thus, what Prudhomme calls "Cajun" does not reflect what Link knows to be Cajun. He also recognizes the fluidity of the definition of Cajun when he writes, "Cajun food has come to mean different things to different people, but as far as I'm concerned it's really a very simple concept: Acadiana is populated by farmers who live off the land, and the cuisine is born of this specific location." Link believes that Cajun food is simply the food eaten by Cajuns in south Louisiana who rely on farming, local sourcing, and sustainability for sustenance. Acknowledging that the essence of Cajun food or Louisiana food is hard to define, Link delivers his own understanding of the regional cuisine as a culinary expression of personal memory.

As early as 1999, Link was breaking down whole hogs and making boudin in the kitchen of his first restaurant, Herbsaint, a modern Creole bistro in New Orleans. The pig-processing practice inspired his second restaurant Cochon (French for pig), which Link defines as "a restaurant that would celebrate authentic Cajun." He uses the word *boucherie* in *Real Cajun*'s description of Cochon but not in reference to the ritual. Instead, he says that the restaurant features an "in-house *boucherie* (butcher shop)." This is important to note because all the other cookbooks examined in this chapter that include the word *boucherie* do so in reference to a communal pig-processing ritual, and not to a meat market. Yet, Link uses the boucherie as ritual as a foundation for the first chapter of *Real Cajun.* The boucherie's imagery, techniques, flavors, and products provide the architecture for his take on pork-based cooking.

Link begins the book with a chapter titled "La Vie Cochon" (The Pig Life), in which he writes: "My most cherished, most powerful food memories involve two ingredients: rice and pork. They're both crucial to Cajun cooking, and while I can't imagine one without the other, no single food embodies the spirit and culture of southwest Louisiana better than the mighty pig." Although the word *boucherie* is not mentioned in the chapter's introduction, the ritual and all its techniques and flavors can be found throughout its pages. "La Vie Cochon" celebrates the life (and death) of the pig and its sacrifice to become the foundation for Link's own version of Cajun food. Link goes on to provide his family history, in which his German ancestors immigrated to Acadia Parish in the late nineteenth century and introduced sausage-smoking techniques to the region's already colorful cuisine. He writes that his family does not cook "stereotypically spicy food" but instead relies on smothering and simmering techniques to maximize flavor extracted from the meat, fat, cartilage, and bones.

Alongside his recipes for bacon, tasso, boudin, "cracklins," smoked sausage, and other pork-based products are photos of community boucheries featuring Black and white butchers and cooks. He also provides instructions that require readers/home cooks to use equipment and ingredients essential to any boucherie, such as sausage stuffers and meat grinders, as well as pig intestines (for sausage casings) and pig's back fat. Link's cooking is tied to the land, to family, to family history, and to memory. He uses this cookbook to capture the sights, flavors, and smells of his childhood; to preserve the threatened land; and to commemorate the colorful foodscape that inspired his own version of Louisiana cuisine.

In *Chasing the Gator: Isaac Toups and the New Cajun Cooking* (2018), Isaac Toups contributes his own perspective to the larger placemaking effort in twenty-first-century Louisiana cookbooks when he writes, "We started cooking what we do out of necessity. But then we decided we liked it, and then traditions were born. Many of those traditions got passed down; some got lost. And then some got revived, like the boucherie. Cajuns were going whole hog way before it was cool."

Toups attributes his own brand of Cajun cooking to his hybrid "Prairie Cajun and Coastal Cajun" upbringing. Like Link, he draws from his childhood observations and familial past to construct the outward-facing cuisine served in his restaurant and outlined in his cookbook. Memory is thus a constant across the canon of contemporary cookbooks in Louisiana and contributes to personal and collective narrative building and placemaking. Chefs and writers today present a more personal, fluid version of Cajun identity that reflects the complexity and multiplicity of Louisiana ethnicities and cuisines.

In *Mosquito Supper Club: Cajun Recipes from a Disappearing Bayou* (2020), Melissa M. Martin offers another chef's take on the intermingling of food and memory in cultural preservation. In this intimate look at her own experience as a Cajun woman and chef, Martin addresses the reader directly and, using the recipe form, constructs a social relationship between readers and herself. She writes about the inseparability of food and memory, about the deep- rootedness of Louisiana's cuisine and literature in the state's oral tradition. By writing the dish into her work, Martin captures an otherwise orally transmitted recipe on the page, allowing the medium of her cookbook to serve as a space for stor(y)ing evanescent moments. She then uses that space to construct her own identity as a chef based on personal and shared experiences.

Yet Martin goes beyond the intimate. Her book functions simultaneously as a politically discursive tool by advocating for a more complex rhetoric surrounding Louisiana food. *Mosquito Supper Club* thus contributes to the contemporary reconstruction of Louisiana cuisine. In "Constructing Ethnicity: Creating and Recreating Ethnic Identity and Culture," Joane Nagel outlines several cultural reconstruction techniques, which include "revivals and restorations of historical cultural practices and institutions." New cultural constructions include "revisions of current culture innovations—the creation of new cultural forms. Cultural symbols, activities, and materials are continually being added to and removed from existing cultural repertoires."

The cultural construction of Martin's text offers a new way of writing about Louisiana cuisine. Her reflections on gumbo are an example of the reinvention of gumbo as a cultural material. Gumbo has stood the test of time as the preferred metaphor for all things Louisiana: its diversity, culture, history, and evolution. It thus goes beyond the Cajun versus Creole debate. For Martin, Louisiana's major waves of immigration can be tasted in almost any bowl of gumbo. She pushes this metaphor even further, to the personal level, when she writes:

> Gumbo represents what's been learned from our ancestors and our communities. Each person cooks one that expresses the way they view food, the culture with which they identify, and their relationship to the food around them. Gumbo is synonymous with Cajun culture, but it would be erroneous to imply that gumbo is solely a Cajun dish. With a past steeped in so many places, gumbo is a personal dish, and each version has a place in the gumbo continuum. It is a multiethnic group project that constantly changes.

This view of cooking cancels out the question of authenticity. For Martin, cooking is not about seeking authenticity; it is about creating something new. Instead of claiming authenticity, she advocates for a more honest look at the past so that food creators can enrich Louisiana cuisine in the present from a personal standpoint. Each dish is unique to its creator in that it contains what can only come from that cook—their memories, emotions, moods, and childhood experiences: their self. Each recipe, oral or written, tells a story about the cook. Just as earlier cookbooks invited the reader to contribute to the experience by cooking the provided recipes, Martin invites the reader to consider their own place on the continuum. She presents the reader with an opportunity to contribute to the evolution of the cuisine. If a reader uses smoked pork sausage in their own gumbo, not only are they participating in the performance of Louisiana culture but they are also actively influencing it, contributing to its development.

The boucherie has, at this point, extended to that reader's kitchen: the personal has become political. When a culture is threatened, the decision to cook a dish while acknowledging the political and cultural exchanges and negotiations that contributed to its development becomes an act of resistance against Americanization. Furthermore, cooking a dish in the present while recognizing its complex past and its place on the continuum of Louisiana cuisine is an act of cultural perpetuation. In personalizing each dish, Martin suggests that each recipe and each time it is prepared represent one point on the perpetually changing continuum of Louisiana cuisine.

This is a revolutionary notion that goes beyond blurring the line between Cajun and Creole: it implies that Louisiana cuisine knows no borders and is only defined by those who cook it and by those who eat it. By revitalizing the way that we think about cooking, Martin and other contemporary food writers engage with the boucherie and its many elements to redefine the meaning of Louisiana cuisine. Such rethinking restructures the discourse surrounding the boucherie and the regional cuisine at large. This shift in discourse sheds new light on Louisiana cuisine and presents an opportunity for a more comprehensive understanding of its history, its culture, and its future.

In *Kevin Belton's Cookin' Louisiana: Flavors from the Parishes of the Pelican State* (2021), this Black Louisiana chef and television personality addresses Louisiana's long-held obsession with locally sourced fresh ingredients when he writes, "While the farm-to-table concept is currently very popular, it was always normal for us." Belton frames Louisiana's culinary history in a non-Acadian-centric context. He offers a narrative that places the evolving cuisine at the center of the story while organizing the Pelican State into five regions. He describes southeast Louisiana as having "a personality of its own . . . because of the variety of people first drawn centuries ago": "Native Americans, French, Spanish, Haitian, Irish, German, and many others." He reminds readers that these groups' "influences are still alive and well in the music, food and architecture of the area."

He describes the central "Crossroads Region" as a sort of gumbo "because it has a mix of cultures that has been simmering for centuries. There's a bit of Spanish, French, African-Ameican, Anglo-American, a dash of Native American, and Cajun ingenuity." Belton assigns the gumbo as an apt metaphor to describe the region's cultural mosaic. From the Native American to the Anglo-American influence on the cuisine, Belton recognizes the evolving nature of food in Louisiana. This acknowledgment of change and continuous development provides a fresh view of Louisiana's culinary past.

Belton relies on personal memory in his presentation of this regional cuisine as he recalls his rural childhood: "As a kid, I was able to see crops growing in the soil, chickens in the coop, pigs in a pen, and cows grazing in the field." By looking back, Belton offers readers a more sustainable, healthy way to live today and in the future. Belton encourages them to shop local, to buy ingredients from farmers' markets and nearby growers. This discourse moves away from the Americanized narrative employed by New Orleans chefs in the 1980s and 1990s toward a more creolized view of the foodscape.

Cookbooks demonstrate the plurality of perspectives in Louisiana in how they discuss the boucherie and other events, symbols, and dishes from Louisiana foodways. Their authors package and export culture in a way that can be commodified and holds monetary value. By preparing the recipes in their cookbooks, readers can purchase access to other cultures and re-create food elements from that culture; the books provide a platform on which readers can construct and express their own cultural identity; and they ultimately serve as a medium for recording memories, experiences, attitudes, and values regarding the cuisine and culture in question. The boucherie, as presented in Louisiana cookbooks, was used by Cajuns to revitalize Cajun culture, and in the process, it presented this culture as the primary culinary and cultural group in Louisiana.

Thus, cookbooks, as a medium, contributed to the marginalization of other cultural groups, especially in the twentieth century. Some notable Cajun chefs came to control the culinary and cultural discourse within and beyond Louisiana, gaining national fame on the backs of Black and Native farmers, butchers, and cooks. By adopting myths like *Évangeline* and names like Acadiana in the early to mid-twentieth century, the important Cajun chefs analyzed in this chapter successfully painted south Louisiana as a white foodscape. They used dishes created primarily by Blacks and Natives to define and export their culture. Their whiteness gave them the privilege to write and disseminate south Louisiana's collective memory, history, and recipes, perhaps unintentionally undermining contributions of people of color.

Ultimately, through cultural preservation efforts, white Cajuns placed themselves at the center of Louisiana's ethnic mosaic by wielding discursive power in the region, controlling cultural knowledge, and claiming the boucherie and other elements of Louisiana food as their own. The boucherie therefore became a racialized and politicized practice.

Twenty-first-century Louisiana chefs have recognized this cultural appropriation and have used the cookbook space to decenter the Cajun perspective and to highlight contributions to the development and evolution of Louisiana food made by marginalized groups, especially Black people and Natives. Through intertwining the personal and the political, contemporary chefs in Louisiana like Martin and Belton join national trends reflected in works like *Choctaw Food: Remembering the Land, Rekindling Ancient Knowledge* by Ian Thompson and *Black Food: Stories, Art, and Recipes from Across the African Diaspora* by Bryant Terry—pushing the cookbook form to new frontiers through poetry, playlists, essays, visual art, and international collaboration to present a fresh way of discussing food, movement, and identity. The cookbook, once a place to gain cultural capital, has become a place of decentering, reclamation, and restoration that is equally about conservation and even more dedicated to conversation.

4

Sauces, Sausages, and Other Ingredients

The Louisiana boucherie underwent drastic changes during the twentieth century. As pigs were found less often on farmsteads and more in the wild or in industrialized slaughterhouses, communal pig slaughtering became more of a niche activity and less of a necessity. Spectacles and visual expressions of Louisiana food became a more important part of the culture after World War II. To enable a better understanding of the omnipresence of the boucherie in Louisiana's cuisine today, this chapter describes the dishes, products, and materials that are part of the boucherie process. The following list is not exhaustive: I chose to leave out fried pig tails, fur (often used as stuffing for pillows), and pig feet or "trotters." Products of boucheries changed, were added, or forsaken at various points throughout their history depending on need, and I include those that are most relevant in today's foodscape.

Fat

The fat of butchered animals has been used for thousands of years for various purposes. One commonality linking all cultures, regions, and animals is that the fat was always processed immediately after butchering; it was separated from the meat and then rendered. Both bear fat, rendered by Indigenous Louisiana communities for thousands of years, and melted pig fat could be used as cooking oil. Cooks used these oils to fry pork or other meats and vegetables, for boiling corn, and for other culinary techniques. Even today at boucheries and in specialty meat markets in Louisiana, pig lard is rendered by cooking fatty chunks of skin slowly, until enough of the fat is rendered into liquid oil. Then, the skin is fried in its own oil until crispy—these crispy chunks of skin are called *gratons,* or cracklings. The remaining lard could be collected and filtered for further use. At my grandfather's meat market in Opelousas, I recall selling pork lard in pint and quart jars.

Pork fat was also rendered into tallow by cutting the raw fat into small pieces and boiling them until the mixture separated into two consistencies: an upper, more solid layer and a lower liquid layer. The harder, upper layer would be scraped and used to make candles or soap. My ancestor Valmar Cormier, mentioned in chapter 2, was interviewed in the 1930s and recounted his experience living as an enslaved child in the 1850s. He said that he grew up mixing this tallow with lye collected from the ashes of a fireplace or wood stove to make soap. The liquid oil can also be used to preserve smoked and salted meats during the cooler months. Many enslaved Blacks

Fatty pork skin cut into cubes for cracklings.

at Louisiana's southeastern plantations were known to burn liquid hog lard in cast-iron kettles to provide light.

Today, one can still find rendered pig fat for sale on the shelves of some specialty meat markets. And of course, it is still the preferred cooking oil for cracklings at some meat markets, restaurants, and boucherie celebrations.

Salt Pork

Salted pork is about as old as the domesticated pig from which it comes. The Romans began salting pork as early as 200 BC. Salting as a curing technique is important in the preservation process. Coarse salt helps remove water from the meat and fat, prolonging the time between slaughter and spoiling. Before curing techniques were developed and made reliable, botulism was a major cause of sickness and death in Europe. Pork lends itself to heavy salting and extensive preservation because of the pig's high fat content. Unlike most other meats, fatty pork retains its tenderness and flavor despite the loss of water.

Although Europeans brought salted pork with them to North America, prehistoric Native Americans already were collecting salt at inland salt licks, processing it, and using it for salting meat and fish that they consumed and traded regionally. The earliest colonists took over and expanded these Native salt works. Salt production and use were local processes. Feral, semi-domesticated, and domesticated swine contributed to diets in rural areas. Salt pork became more popular in urban Louisiana once centralized slaughterhouses and meat markets became common in cities like New Orleans.

By the mid-nineteenth century, salt pork was the primary meat-based protein in Louisiana diets. As mentioned earlier, corn-based dishes like couche-couche (which probably derived from North African couscous) contained salt pork, and most enslaved Blacks, *petits habitants,* German immigrants, and poor Creole farmers survived the winters thanks in large part to a hearty blend of salt pork and corn.

Although salted pork is not as popular as boudin today, it remains an important flavoring agent for dishes eaten as sides in restaurants, homes, and at boucheries throughout south Louisiana. Field peas, green beans, black-eyed peas, purple-hull peas, and baked beans are among the many sides that begin by first frying salted pork—such as bacon (salted pork belly fat), ham (salted shoulder or rump), or salted shank meat—in cooking oil with onions and then adding the peas or beans. Therefore, the boucherie's influence on Louisiana's cuisine does not stop at contemporary exhibitions of the ritual; staple dishes demonstrate the importance of its products to Louisiana cuisine at large.

Boudin

Boudin is one of Louisiana's most important food staples. It is revered by Louisianans from many ethnic and cultural groups in south Louisiana, who often recommend it to tourists and visitors. As a displaced Louisianan, I miss boudin more than most other food items.

In *Stir the Pot: The History of Cajun Cuisine* (2005), Marcelle Bienvenu, Carl A. Brasseaux, and Ryan A. Brasseaux write that the term *boudin* first appeared in thirteenth-century northern France to describe blood sausage. A French word, it derives from the word *bédaine,* meaning belly, guts, or entrails. Since then, boudin has contained meat, entrails, and lots of fat. Louisiana boudin still contains a fair amount of fat, whether eaten freshly made at a boucherie or purchased from a specialty meat market. Popular books on Cajun cuisine, like *Stir the Pot* and *Cajun Pig,* almost unfailingly provide descriptions of Louisiana's two main types of boudin: *boudin noir* and *boudin blanc.*

This unique sausage consists of a cooked and ground mixture of pork meat, fat, often liver and other organs, and rice, which is stuffed into pig intestines. *Boudin noir,* or blood boudin, is made by mixing these ingredients with the animal's freshly drained blood, known colloquially as "swine brine." The small intestines are cleaned out by soaking and scrubbing in hot water and baking soda. Rice entered the sausage shortly after Louisiana rice cultivation dramatically increased in the early nineteenth century. It was a cheap, widely available filler that would allow farmers to use less pork per boudin link.

The boudin made at boucheries from the nineteenth to twenty-first centuries hardly resembles the sausages known as *boudin* or *boudin blanc* in France. Although its name is French, boudin is a sausage born in French America. Late seventeenth- and early eighteenth-century boudin in French Canada and Louisiana consisted of buffalo meat, fat, and kidney suet stuffed into buffalo intestines and fried in bear fat. Native Americans were then preparing and eating similar butchered products using intestines and other entrails as casing. West Africans introduced rice and braising techniques to the sausage. By the late eighteenth century, Louisianans were eating less bear and buffalo and more pigs and cattle, and by the turn of the nineteenth century, Louisiana boudin was starting to resemble its contemporary version.

Today, boudin can be found smoked, stuffed with cheese and deep fried, and pan fried in egg rolls, pies, sandwiches, cakes, and in virtually any other form imaginable. Cauliflower has even replaced rice in some outlets. At Opelousas's annual beef cookoff, beef boudin is inevitably a contender. No matter which form boudin takes, it represents its complex history of creolization.

Smoked and Fresh Sausage

Smoked sausage remains a staple product of today's boucheries and most specialty meat markets in south Louisiana. However, it was not a part of Louisiana cuisine until the arrival of German immigrants. Just as smoked sausages were important features of annual German Schlachtfests and today's Oktoberfests, the Louisiana boucherie exhibits south Germany's culinary influence on the Lower Mississippi Valley since the turn of the eighteenth century. In Germany, nearly all smoked meats are cooked over oak wood. In Louisiana, indigenous woods, including that of the Mockernut Hickory and various types of pecan and oak trees, were and are still used to smoke sausages during boucheries.

Since the first wave of German immigrants arrived in Louisiana, smokehouses and smoking techniques have evolved and taken many forms. Louisianans have smoked meats by placing them above smoky fires, in the open, in earth ovens, in smokehouses converted from chicken coops and sweet-potato curing houses, and in other ways. Smokehouses were typically made of wood until the introduction of tin and steel to Louisiana. Today, most smokehouses are made of stainless steel or cast iron. No matter the material, the method of smoking today resembles that of both early German immigrants and

Indigenous Louisianans: a fire is lit and then smothered with ashes or wood chips, and the meat is hung either above or next to the smoke in a smokehouse, earth oven, or in the open.

Early smoked sausages contained minimal ingredients: pork, salt, and fat ground and stuffed into pig intestines. Like all things, the dish evolved to contain more complex mixtures such as pork and beef, pork and chicken, and pork and venison, all with varying levels of fat and spices such as pepper and salt. The smoked sausages described earlier and andouille sausage remain part of the Louisiana boucherie. The main difference between the two is that andouille, along with pork meat, contains chopped intestines, stomach, and other digestive organs. Andouille was typically stuffed into the large intestines and therefore tended to be larger in circumference than other smoked sausages and boudin, which were stuffed into small intestines.

According to *Stir the Pot,* one of the earliest records of andouille being made in Louisiana came from the German Coast (today's St. Charles and St. John the Baptist Parishes). In addition to smoking sausage, fresh sausage also derived from the boucherie ritual, contains similar ingredient variations as the smoked variety, and is often found in more traditional meat markets today.

Tasso

Tasso (or *tasseau*) is another smoked meat that remains a staple in Cajun food discourse. Although it is no longer commonly made during boucheries, it has a relatively long history. Tasso—known today as smoked pork shoulder steaks—for most of its history was made from buffalo or beef. Thinly sliced strips of beef or bison would be seasoned with salt and sometimes pepper and cured for days, usually in the summer. They were sometimes hung in the sun all day to dry in the intense heat or were preserved by smoking. I once learned during a long and rich conversation with Ray Brassieur, a relative of mine and fellow Louisiana ethnographer, that Choctaw and other Indigenous groups such as the northern Cree tribes introduced this method of preservation to French frontiersmen. These groups smoked fish, venison, bison, and more, flavoring the meat with bear fat, fruits, nuts, and salt. This mixture was known as *pémican,* or pemmican.

Tasso was especially popular in the prairie region of south-central Louisiana, where cattle were more often raised. However, after the Civil War, Louisiana's crippled economy forced many ranchers into sharecropping. It is at this period that records show a shift from beef to pork as the common ingredient for smoked or cured tasso. Today, like ham, bacon, and salt pork, tasso is used to season beans and peas. It is also used in gumbo and other soups to add a rich, smoky flavor. Tasso serves as another example of the ritual's ubiquitous impact on Louisiana cuisine.

Panse/Chaudin

Another commonly smoked dish is called *panse* (alternate spelling *ponce*), which the *Dictionary of Louisiana French* defines as the stomach of a cow or pig that is prepared as food. When the word *panse* is used alone, it usually refers to a pig's stomach, and *panse de bête* (tripe) specifically describes a cow's stomach. Like the intestines used for sausage making, the stomach was cleaned out by soaking and scrubbing in hot water and baking soda. In boucheries from the nineteenth to twenty-first centuries, the *panse* is stuffed with the same mixture used to fill smoked sausages: ground pork, fat, salt, and other seasonings. Once stuffed, the *panse* is either cooked immediately in a gravy on a stovetop or baked. Baked stuffed *panse* is known as *chaudin.* If the stomach is stuffed and smoked, it is known either as *panse bourée* or *panse boucanée.* The stomach was smoked in the same manner used to preserve sausages, so Native peoples and Franco-Germans are both responsible for the development of *panse* as a Louisiana dish.

My mom grew up in Eunice and recalls eating panse at family holiday gatherings. For her, this is a comfort food. She still sometimes cooks it around Thanksgiving by braising the smoked stomach in oil with vegetables and serving it in its sauce over rice. This method is another example of West African contributions to the boucherie. *Panse* was and remains more commonly eaten in the central prairie region of Louisiana, where more pig and cattle husbandry were practiced than in other regions.

Hog's Head Cheese

Hog's head cheese is reminiscent of France's country pâté. Both dishes are made by blending gelatinous pork with spices. In Louisiana, it has been prepared and consumed as long as pigs have lived in the region. For most of this time, it has primarily consisted of boiled pig's head and feet. Once thoroughly boiled, the mixture is allowed to cool. A gelatinous substance rises to the top of the liquid, which comes from the collagen in the pig's head and feet. This gelatin is

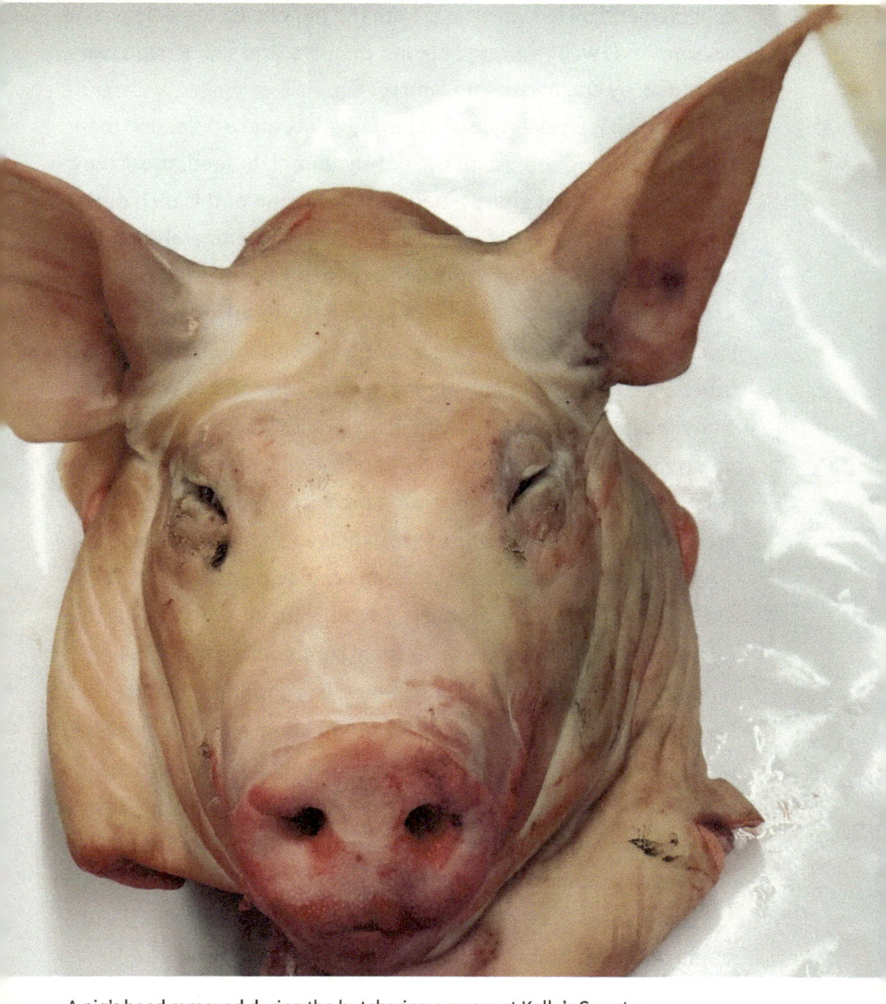

A pig's head removed during the butchering process at Kelly's Country Meat Block.

collected and mixed with meat from the pig's head, lower legs, and elsewhere, as well as ground onions, peppers, and salt. Recipes vary, of course, by era, household, and region.

The dish is an example of Cajun ingenuity and a reflection of the cuisine's valuing the use of the entire animal. Indeed, most pork-consuming cultural groups made some version of this dish during their own boucheries before the introduction of refrigeration. Some boucheries still involve the making and eating of hog's head cheese. At an annual family boucherie that I used to attend in Maurice, Louisiana, the host's mother-in-law simply brought hog's head cheese purchased from the Piggly Wiggly in Scott. The dish is sold in specialty meat markets, but as with French pâtés, contemporary hog's head cheese consists of mostly pork and fat, which is held together by gelatin purchased separately by the producer and added to a finely ground seasoned pork mixture to resemble more traditional versions.

Hog's head cheese is a traditional Acadian dish. In *Pantry & Palate,* Acadian chef and food writer Simon Thibault provides a recipe for Acadian hog's head cheese. German communities also consumed it during and after their own boucheries. It is important to note that, like all other boucherie products of antebellum Louisiana, enslaved Black workers were the primary butchers and cooks on farmsteads in Louisiana. Therefore, the development of French country pâté into Louisiana's uniquely spicy hog's head cheese can be attributed to Afro-Creole culinary ingenuity.

Head cheese is eaten more as a novelty today and is less of a staple than dishes like boudin and smoked sausage.

Débris

The next dish goes by several names, all found in the *Dictionary of Louisiana French: débris du cochon, bouilli, fressures,* or, in English, cowboy stew. Each of these terms describes the same dish: pork entrails braised in cooking oil along with peppers, onions, and other vegetables and then eaten as a stew over rice. The organs usually included the kidneys, lungs, pancreas, heart, liver, and gallbladder. They would be fried in oil before adding onions, peppers, and sometimes celery or garlic; then water would be added to slowly cook the mixture down into a dark gravy. Like hog's head cheese, this dish reflects a dedication to using as much of the animal as possible.

Organs contain little fat and lots of water and therefore cannot be very well preserved, so *débris* was usually eaten the day that the pig was killed. Because boucheries lasted an entire day and into the night, someone would be cooking *débris* to fuel the butchers as they worked. Today, because of health concerns, only a few slaughterhouses in south Louisiana sell the entrails needed to cook this dish. Therefore, *débris* is typically only eaten at boucheries or in the homes of a few dedicated cooks. This dish survives almost exclusively because of boucheries, which is likely a result of the widened accessibility of more "desirable" cuts of meat.

Backbone Stew: What the Butchers Eat

West African cooking pervades nearly every pot at any boucherie held today. Some noteworthy dishes found at today's boucheries and at many restaurants selling Cajun food are backbone stew, pork stew, smothered pork chops, smothered pork ribs, fried pork ribs, gumbo, pork *grillades,* smoked sausage in a red gravy, and pork roast. Each of these dishes contains either braised pork or pork boiled in gravy, and all are served over rice. Like *débris,* backbone stew was often cooked on the same day that the pigs were killed and fueled the hardworking butchers.

Although gumbo is not often connected to boucheries in contemporary scholarship, it often contains smoked sausage, andouille, and smoked tasso. Its primary protein source and flavoring agents often come from or are inspired by boucheries.

Michael Twitty celebrates the West African presence in Louisiana cuisine: "The heart of southern Louisiana cuisine, Creole or Cajun, is the roux, the thickening mother sauce brought from France three centuries ago. It can come in as many colors as the people you see on the streets of New Orleans. Each presents the main ingredients in a different way and these become the dishes we rave; they are laced with the holy trinity of bell peppers, onions, and tomatoes (some say green onions, some say garlic) that is as Senegalese as they come, or Dahoman or Kongolese."

Backbone stew is made by almost burning pieces of the backbone—meat from the spine that is cut into chops or cubes—in cooking oil. The idea is to brown the meat in a heavy pot over high heat so that bits of skin, fat, meat, and gristle stick to the bottom. Once all the meat is golden brown, the cook adds onions, peppers, and maybe celery and garlic. These vegetables, after being introduced to the high

Opposite: A butcher at the Maurice boucherie stirring the beginnings of a stew.

heat, will release much of their water and deglaze the bottom of the pot, thereby beginning the stew. After frying the vegetables, water or stock is added. It is at this point that today's cook might add roux from a jar to thicken the stew, although a more dedicated cook might have begun with a roux. Either way, the roux is crucial for achieving the thickness that allows us to call this a stew (and not a sauce or gumbo). The cook lets the stew simmer, tastes, adds seasoning, and tastes again. When their ancestor whispers in their ear saying, "That's enough, sha," they will call it done.

* * *

Since Louisiana's first inhabitants came to the Lower Mississippi Valley more than twelve thousand years ago, the boucherie and its meat-processing rituals and practices have evolved from the killing, processing, and consumption of peccaries, buffalo, bear, deer, and hogs for sustenance and tallow-based products to serving as a celebration of Louisiana culture. After the introduction of refrigeration technology to the region, the boucherie's sustenance function became virtually obsolete. However, it evolved into a spectacle of cultural expression. Cajuns use the boucherie along with other culinary events such as the *cochon de lait* and cookoffs to define and express their cultural identity.

Today, as butchers, cooks, or attendees, we perform this cultural ritual that brings people together, often from different cultures and backgrounds. Despite increasing pressures to eat plant-based foods, the boucherie lives on as a communal performance, a collective re-actualization of a past necessity. It celebrates cultural diversity and sparks a shift from conservation of sustenance to conversations of culinary and social values.

The boucherie is a multidimensional, plural, and ever-evolving spectacle of diversity and culinary ingenuity, a glimpse into the past(s) that informs our present and helps create our future. Given its unique variety of endogenous and exogenous influences and ingredients, the boucherie is performed still today as a spectacle that nourishes Louisiana's foodscape at the intersection of localization and globalization.

sources

Bass, S. Jonathan. "How 'bout a Hand for the Hog: The Enduring Nature of the Swine as a Cultural Symbol in the South." *Southern Cultures* 1, no. 3 (1995): 301–20.

Belton, Kevin. *Kevin Belton's Cookin' Louisiana: Flavors from the Parishes of the Pelican State.* Gibbs Smith, 2021.

Bernard, Shane. *The Cajuns: Americanization of a People.* University Press of Mississippi, 2003.

Bienvenu, Marcelle, Carl Brasseaux, and Ryan Brasseaux. *Stir the Pot: A History of Cajun Cuisine.* Hippocrene Books, 2005.

Creole Cajun Cookery. Daily Iberian, 1952.

Essig, Mark. *Lesser Beasts: A Snout-to-Tail History of the Humble Pig.* Basic Books, 2015.

Folse, John D., and George Rodrigue. *The Encyclopedia of Cajun & Creole Cuisine.* Chef John Folse & Company Pub., 2004.

Hall, Gwendolyn Midlo. *Africans in Colonial Louisiana: The Development of Afro-Creole Culture in the Eighteenth Century.* LSU Press, 1995.

Harris, Jessica. *High on the Hog: A Culinary Journey from Africa to America.* Bloomsbury, 2011.

Hawkins, Nancy W., and Robert W. Neuman. *Louisiana Prehistory.* Department of Culture, Recreation and Tourism, Louisiana Archaeological Survey and Antiquities Commission, Anthropological Study no. 6, 2024.

Link, Donald. *Real Cajun: Rustic Home Cooking from Donald Link's Louisiana.* Clarkson Potter, 2009.

Martin, Melissa M. *Mosquito Supper Club: Cajun Recipes from a Disappearing Bayou.* Artisan, 2020.

McDermott, John Francis. *A Glossary of Mississippi Valley French, 1673–1850.* Washington University, 1941.

McIntyre, William G. *Prehistoric Indian Settlements of the Changing Mississippi River Delta.* LSU Press, 1958.

Michot, Ashlee Wilson, ed. *Ô Malheureuse: French Writings by Louisiana Women.* UL Press, 2019.

Nagel, Joane. "Constructing Ethnicity: Creating and Recreating Ethnic Identity and Culture." *Social Problems* 41, no. 1 (1994): 152–76.

Poché, Dixie. *Cajun Pig: Boucheries, Cochon de Laits and Boudin.* Arcadia Publishing, 2020.

Prudhomme, Paul. *Chef Prudhomme's Louisiana Kitchen.* HarperCollins, 1984.

———. *The Prudhomme Family Cookbook: Old-Time Louisiana Recipes.* 1987.

———. *Chef Paul Prudhomme's Taste of Louisiana.* Morrow, 2000.

Sibley, J. Ashley. *Louisiana's Ancients of Man: A Study of Changing Characteristics of Louisiana Indian Cultures, Including a Glossary of Anthropological and Archaeological Terms.* Claitor's Publishing, 1967.

Terry, Bryant. *Black Food Stories, Art, and Recipes from Across the African Diaspora.* 4 Color Books, 2021.

Thibault, Simon. *Pantry and Palate: Remembering and Rediscovering Acadian Food.* Nimbus Pub. Ltd., 2017.

Thompson, Ian. *Choctaw Food: Remembering the Land, Rekindling Ancient Knowledge.* Choctaw Nation of Oklahoma, 2019.

Toups, Isaac. *Chasing the Gator: Isaac Toups and the New Cajun Cooking.* Voracious, 2018.

Trépanier, Cécyle. "The Cajunization of French Louisiana: Forging a Regional Identity." *Geographical Journal* 157, no. 2 (1991): 161–71.

Twitty, Michael W. *The Cooking Gene: A Journey Through African American Culinary History in the Old South.* HarperCollins, 2017.

Usner, Daniel H. *Indians, Settlers, and Slaves in a Frontier Exchange Economy: The Lower Mississippi Valley Before 1783.* University of North Carolina Press, 1992.

Valdman, Albert, Kevin J. Rotter, Barry Jean Ancelet, Richard Guidry, et al. *Dictionary of Louisiana French: As Spoken in Cajun, Creole, and American Indian Communities* University Press of Mississippi, 2009.
Wilson, Kurt M., and Matthew G. Hill. "Synthesis and Assessment of the Flat-Headed Peccary Record in North America." *Quaternary Science Reviews* 248 (2020). https://www.sciencedirect.com/science/article/pii/S0277379120305631#abs0015.